HISTORICAL FACTS

WORLD WAR II

Earlier types of Britain's Churchill tank, like this Mark
II of c.1942, were heavily armoured but under gunned.

The North American
P-51 Mustang (top) was one of the most important fighters
of the war. With droppable fuel tanks (as seen here), it
could escort British-based bombers on raids deep into Germany.

Mounting some 13 defensive machine guns, the Boeing
B-17 bomber was named the 'Flying Fortress'. It bore
the brunt of the U.S.A.A.F.'s attack on Germany.

HISTORICAL FACTS
WORLD WAR II

RICHARD O'NEILL

Grange
BOOKS

CLB 2839

© 1992 Colour Library Books Ltd., Godalming, Surrey, England.

Published by Grange Books
An Imprint of Grange Books Limited
The Grange
Grange Yard
London
SE1 3AG

Published 1993

ISBN 1 85627 389 X

Printed and bound in Italy

The Author

Richard O'Neill was born in Northampton, England. He has been a soldier, professional boxer, labourer, actor, and writer of fiction, comic strips, and stage and television plays. In recent years he has specialized in historical non-fiction. His book *Suicide Squads: Special Attack Weapons of World War II* was published in Britain and the U.S.A. in 1981, and in Japan in 1988. He is co-author of two books on toy collecting, and has edited and contributed to many books on military history and weaponry. He was a major contributor to *Lands and Peoples,* a multi-volume work published in the U.S.A. and other countries in 1990-92. He is currently writing a book on the Middle Ages, two books on ghosts, monsters and similar phenomena, and working on a movie project with his son Danny, an actor and director.

Credits

Editor: Richard O'Neill
Designer: Jill Coote
Map artwork: Peter Bull
Picture Editor: Miriam Sharland
Production: Ruth Arthur, Sally Connolly, Andrew Whitelaw
Director of Production: Gerald Hughes
Typesetting: SX Composing Ltd.
Colour separations: Advance Laser Graphics Ltd., Hong Kong
Printed and bound by New Interlitho SpA, Italy

An R.A.F. air gunner in training on the ground prepares to squeeze the pistol grips of a twin mounted machine gun. The 7.92mm or 0.303in machine gun was standard defensive armament on most British bombers.

CONTENTS

Introduction

World War II means different things to different nations. For Britain and most European countries it began in September 1939, with Germany's invasion of Poland. For the U.S.S.R., the 'Great Patriotic War' began with the German invasion of June 1941. For the U.S.A. it began in December 1941, with Japan's attack on Pearl Harbor. For Japan and China it may be said to have begun as early as 1937, when Japan struck south from its puppet state in Manchuria to begin the Sino-Japanese War of 1937-45.

Chinese resistance was hampered by internal strife between the Nationalist forces led by Generalissimo Chiang Kai-shek (1887-1975) and the Communist guerrillas of Marshal Chu Teh (1886-1976) and Mao Tse-tung (1893-1976). Europe also saw 'wars within the War'. In Yugoslavia, Royalist 'Chetniks' led by General Draza Mihailovich (1893-1946) fought as fiercely against the Communist 'partisans' of Marshal (Josip Broz) Tito (1892-1980) as both 'Chetniks' and 'partisans' fought against the German invader.

Clashes between Communist and non-Communist resistance movements threatened to escalate into civil war in France in 1944 – and did so in Greece immediately after its liberation in 1944-45.

These 'sideshows' were perhaps more important to those who fought in them than the global struggle between the great powers. But they can receive only passing mention in this book, where I have tried to give the non-specialist reader an overall picture of World War II by describing some two score 'highlights' or 'turning points'.

In the opening pages I have summarized the political and economic events that brought Hitler,

Headline news in London on September 3, 1939: Britain and France declare war against Hitler's Germany.

The 'Big Three' Allied leaders seen in 1945: British premier Churchill; U.S. President Franklin D. Roosevelt; and Soviet dictator Josef Stalin.

German dictator Hitler looks grimly determined in 1938.

Italian dictator Benito Mussolini, Hitler's partner under the Rome-Berlin 'Axis' pact of 1936, rides in triumph through Rome with his ally.

Mussolini and the Japanese warlords to power. Thereafter I have described some of the most significant campaigns of World War II; in each case trying to give the reader a clear idea of why and how actions were fought, who were the commanders and what were their forces, why they resulted as they did, and what were their consequences. I hope that my brief accounts may inspire the reader to seek out far more detailed descriptions, for I believe that we should all have some knowledge of these great events that shaped the world we now inhabit.

World War II was the first and only 'global war', involving almost every sovereign state in the world. Among the few nations to remain neutral throughout were Switzerland (the world's financial centre), Sweden (whose neutrality was similarly of economic value to both sides), the Irish Republic, Spain and Portugal with their African possessions, Afghanistan, Yemen, Nepal and Mongolia.

Some nations fought on both sides. Italy was a founder member of the 'Axis' (Mussolini called the Italian-German pact of 1936 an 'axis' round which their common interests revolved), but after surrendering to the Allies in 1943 quickly declared war on Germany. Vichy (non-occupied) France was virtually Germany's ally in 1940-43. Bulgaria joined the Axis in March 1941, fought against Yugoslavia, Greece and the U.S.S.R., but changed sides in September 1944. Romania played a major part in the invasion of the U.S.S.R. (as did Hungary); then fought against Germany from August 1944. Finland fought and lost its 'Winter War' against the U.S.S.R. in 1939-40; joined Germany in the invasion of the U.S.S.R. in 1941; then joined the Allies in September 1944. In the Far East, Japanese controlled governments in Siam (Thailand) and Burma (Myanmar) declared war on the Allies, but late in the war aided them against the Japanese.

I WANT YOU
for the U.S. ARMY

Reviving a famous image of World War I, 'Uncle Sam' calls for volunteers for a second world conflict.

Women, like this group of snipers seen on the East Front in 1945, played a full combat role in the huge fighting forces of the U.S.S.R.

On the swastika flag of the Third Reich, German army recruits in 1933 swear an oath of loyalty to Hitler and fatherland.

The major Allied nations were Britain and her Commonwealth (then still called the British Empire, and including Canada, India, Australia, New Zealand and South Africa), China, and, from 1941, the U.S.S.R. (which did not join the fight against Japan until August 1945) and the U.S.A. They were joined by almost every nation unmentioned so far: from Costa Rica and Cuba, which declared war on the Axis in December 1941, to Turkey, which delayed its declaration until March 1945. Brazil and Mexico contributed notable combat units to the Allied cause, on whose side the 'Fighting French', 'Free Poles', and servicemen and women who had escaped from other occupied countries – notably Czechoslovakia, Denmark and Holland – did gallant service.

There were two major reasons for the Allied victory: the industrial might of the U.S.A., and the fortitude of the men and women of the huge fighting forces of the U.S.S.R. Pages of statistics could support this statement – but a few must suffice (all figures are approximate). The peak strength of Germany's armed forces was 10,000,000, and of Japan's 6,000,000. The U.S.S.R.'s peak strength was 20,000,000 (and that of the U.S.A. more than 16,000,000). Germany produced 119,000 military aircraft in 1939-45 and Japan 60,000; the U.S.A. produced 272,000 in 1940-45; the U.S.S.R. 158,000; Britain 129,000.

Germany produced 43,000 armoured fighting vehicles; the U.S.A. more than 90,000 – and the U.S.S.R., its war industries relocated beyond the range of the Luftwaffe, which failed to develop heavy bombers, about 100,000. Excluding landing craft, the U.S.A. completed 8,800 warships, including 27 heavy and 111 light aircraft carriers and 870 destroyers and destroyer escorts; Japan built fewer than 1,000.

The Allies' other great advantage lay in their leaders. Whatever their faults, British premier

Winston Churchill (1874-1965) and President Franklin D. Roosevelt (1882-1945) were able to inspire their peoples to victory. They usually made the right decisions – notably that to concentrate major force on the defeat of Germany before bringing full pressure to bear on Japan – and, just as importantly, trusted their military commanders to carry them out without undue interference. Among the greatest Allied commanders were Britain's Field Marshals Harold Alexander (1891-1969), Bernard Montgomery (1887-1976) and William Slim (1891-1970); the U.S.A.'s Generals of the Army Dwight D. Eisenhower (1890-1969) and Douglas MacArthur (1880-1964), and, unmatched as a 'fighting' leader, General George S. Patton (1885-1945); and the U.S.S.R.'s Marshal Georgi Zhukov (1896-1974). I will single out for special mention General of the Army George C. Marshall (1880-1959), who as U.S. Army Chief of Staff, 1939-45, was perhaps the greatest 'planner of victory', and whose post-war 'Marshall Plan' helped rebuild western Europe.

As U.S. Army Chief of Staff, General George C. Marshall was an architect of victory.

Informally dressed and at ease, Winston Churchill relaxes in characteristic style – with a good cigar.

U.S.S. *Missouri*, the last American battleship to enter service (still active in the 1990s), prepares for her first cruise in 1944.

The durable Curtiss P-40 Warhawk was one of the war's most widely used fighter-bombers; around 12,000 saw service.

Adolf Hitler (1889-1945) also inspired his nation – but to destruction. His attack on the U.S.S.R. was a blunder on a scale only approached by Japan's attack (and failure fully to follow through that attack) on Pearl Harbor. Both 'wakened a sleeping giant' whose revenge was terrible. Germany's best commanders – among them Field Marshals Fritz von Manstein (1887-1973), Erwin Rommel (1891-1944), Albert Kesselring (1885-1960), and General Heinz Guderian (1888-1954) – were fatally handicapped by Hitler's constant interference. Japan's war effort suffered from bitter rivalry between Army and Navy leaders: premier General Hideki Tojo (1884-1948) failed to give the tough leadership needed so that war plans might be properly coordinated, and even 'exiled' his best commander, General Tomoyuki Yamashita (1885-1946), to a non-vital post in China in 1942-44, fearing him as a political rival.

It is generally accepted that World War II cost more than 50,000,000 lives. (The following figures are approximate.) The U.S.S.R. lost 13,600,000 military personnel and 7,000,000 civilians; China 1,500,000 military – and perhaps 20,000,000 civilians. Germany's military loss was 3,500,000, with 2,000,000 civilians; Japan lost 2,600,000 military and 950,000 civilians. Poland's losses were 600,000 military and 6,000,000 civilians (including 3,000,000 Jews). Yugoslavia had 305,000 military dead and 1,400,000 civilians. The U.S.A. lost 292,000 military (fewer than in the Civil War); Britain and her Commonwealth, 373,000 military (fewer than in World War I) and 93,000 civilians. In considering the statistics, we must remember the suffering they conceal: millions left physically or mentally crippled, starving or homeless; millions

New life in the midst of death. A G.I. on Saipan holds a tiny baby; miraculous survivor of mass suicide by Japanese troops and civilians.

War's end – and the survivors view the ruins. This was the state to which Hitler's dream of conquest had reduced many European cities by 1945.

A concentration camp survivor mourns over fragments of bone raked from the incinerators – all that is left of many of his fellow sufferers.

trapped behind the 'Iron Curtain' (not lifted until the 1990s) of Communism in eastern Europe; millions who died in wars of 'independence', from Indonesia to Greece, and in partitioned Korea and Vietnam, stemming directly from the events of 1939-45.

World War II changed human society more profoundly than any other event in history. Even had Christ, Muhammad and the Buddha never lived, humankind would have maintained religious belief. The fall of the Roman Empire plunged the West into the so called 'Dark Ages', but from these the medieval world emerged with the ancient certainties intact. But World War II destroyed humanity's belief in its ability to achieve its greatest ideals. Although the forces of 'freedom' and 'democracy' triumphed, the certainties of moral and spiritual progress towards a perfect society were burned in the ovens of Auschwitz, buried under the ruins of Dresden and blotted out by the mushroom-shaped cloud over Hiroshima.

Hitler's rise to power

Mutinies and strikes at home, rather than defeat in battle, forced Germany to accept Allied terms for ending World War I on November 11, 1918. Many Germans believed their country had been 'stabbed in the back' by Communists and corrupt businessmen (many of whom, right-wing extremists said, were Jewish). Left-wing risings in Berlin and elsewhere were put down by paramilitary 'Free Corps' of combat veterans. Both rightists and leftists attacked the Weimar Republic (the moderately socialist national government), especially when inflation fuelled by Allied demands for heavy compensation for war damages made German currency near worthless in 1921-23. One of Weimar's fiercest opponents was Adolf Hitler, who in April 1920 formed the National Socialist German Workers' Party (N.S.D.A.P.; 'Nazis'). By 1932, Hitler's rabble-rousing promises of a 'Greater Germany', and the ruthless suppression of opposition by his brown-shirted 'Storm Troopers' (S.A.), had won the N.S.D.A.P. a majority in the *Reichstag* (German parliament). Hitler became Chancellor in January 1933 and, playing on fear of Communism, dictator in 1934. Although the Versailles Treaty of 1919 limited Germany's army and forbade her warplanes and other 'offensive' weapons, Hitler quickly built up his armed forces. He used the Spanish Civil War (1936-39), in which planes of his 'Condor Legion' helped the right-wing forces of General Franco to victory, as a test ground for new weapons and tactics.

The swastika banner: an ever present symbol in Hitler's Germany.

'Hold high the banner,' began the Nazi anthem. The young soldier who proudly holds it here wears a lanyard awarded for good marksmanship on the breast of his tunic.

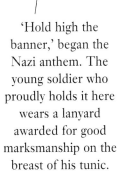

Hitler's uniform during army manoeuvres in 1938 features the medal of the Iron Cross (1st Class), awarded to him as a corporal in World War I.

Children of German-speaking inhabitants of the Sudetenland give Hitler a rapturous welcome in 1938, when the area was grabbed from Czechoslavakia.

Marking a major step in the build up of Germany's military might, the battle cruiser *Scharnhorst* is launched in late 1936.

The straight arm salute, with the words *'Heil Hitler!'* was the Nazi greeting.

Standing in his impressive Mercedes automobile, Hitler returns the salute.

WH-32288

❏ Hitler, whose bullying father had changed the family name from Shicklgrüber in 1876, had a tough early life. His beloved mother died when he was 18; he starved as a would-be artist in Vienna; and in World War I, when as an N.C.O. he won the Iron Cross (1st Class), he was wounded, gassed and temporarily blinded.

❏ In November 1923, Hitler's N.S.D.A.P. tried to overthrow the Bavarian government. The Munich 'Beer Hall Putsch' was easily put down and Hitler was given five years' jail. He served only a few months in a comfortable castle, where he wrote *Mein Kampf* ('My Struggle').

❏ The S.A., the private army that helped Hitler to power, was seen by the German Army as a rival. To consolidate his Army support, Hitler destroyed the S.A. on the 'Night of the Long Knives', June 30-July 1, 1934. S.A. commander Ernst Röhm and many of his comrades were executed. The 'Blackshirts' of the S.S., headed by Heinrich Himmler (above), supplanted the 'Brownshirts' of the S.A.

Caesar in a black shirt

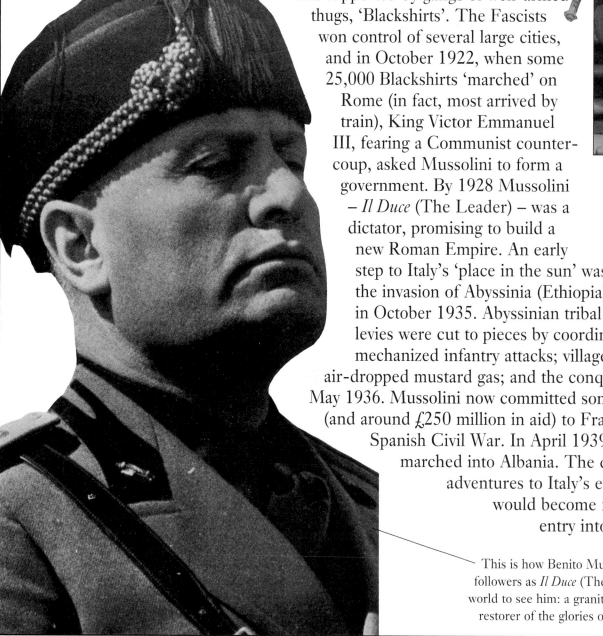

Italy, although one of the victors, suffered heavily in World War I and was disappointed by her meagre territorial gains. One of the loudest voices of discontent belonged to Benito Mussolini, a wounded veteran and former left-wing journalist. In March 1919, in Milan, he founded the *Fasci di Combattimento* (Fascist) movement. It was ultra-nationalist, and its economic programme, the 'corporate state', involved state control over all industry and services at the cost of personal freedom. Like Hitler, Mussolini was a brilliant orator and was supported by gangs of well-armed thugs, 'Blackshirts'. The Fascists won control of several large cities, and in October 1922, when some 25,000 Blackshirts 'marched' on Rome (in fact, most arrived by train), King Victor Emmanuel III, fearing a Communist counter-coup, asked Mussolini to form a government. By 1928 Mussolini – *Il Duce* (The Leader) – was a dictator, promising to build a new Roman Empire. An early step to Italy's 'place in the sun' was the invasion of Abyssinia (Ethiopia) in October 1935. Abyssinian tribal levies were cut to pieces by coordinated air and mechanized infantry attacks; villages were depopulated by air-dropped mustard gas; and the conquest was completed by May 1936. Mussolini now committed some 50,000 'volunteers' (and around £250 million in aid) to Franco's cause in the Spanish Civil War. In April 1939 Italian troops marched into Albania. The damage done by these adventures to Italy's economy and morale would become fully apparent after her entry into World War II.

Hermann Goering, German air chief.

The eagle, symbol of Imperial Rome, features on Mussolini's uniform.

This is how Benito Mussolini – known to his followers as *Il Duce* (The Leader) – liked the world to see him: a granite jawed 'superman', restorer of the glories of Ancient Rome.

The tasselled cap worn by this Italian soldier marks him as a member of an elite *Bersaglieri* (light infantry) unit. Many Italians did not favour the alliance with Germany.

Count Ciano, Italy's Foreign Minister.

Behind and to the left of Hitler stands Rudolf Hess, Deputy Leader of Germany from 1933. In 1941 he flew to Britain, perhaps on a 'peace mission'.

Mussolini, a rabble-rousing journalist not yet 40 years old, prepares to take control of Italy in October 1922. He promised his countrymen 'a place in the sun', but led them to defeat.

Black-shirted paramilitary thugs — many of them discontented ex-soldiers of World War I, like the bemedalled veteran here — brought Mussolini to power in the 'March on Rome'.

War lords of the east

Japan's transformation in the 1860s-1920s from an isolated, backward state to a great industrial and military power astonished the world. But by the 1920s the nation faced potential crisis: a population explosion threatened to swamp the Japanese home islands, which, lacking natural resources, were heavily dependent on imported raw materials. Japan felt herself threatened by Western nations who could, by economic blockade, curb her expansion. Many politicians and military men concluded that Japan's only option was to force its oil and mineral rich neighbours into a Japanese-dominated 'Greater East Asian Co-Prosperity Sphere'. Since Army and Navy Ministers had to be serving officers, the services could bring down any government that opposed military imperialism. The people were conditioned for the forthcoming struggle by 'State Shinto', an ultra-nationalistic updating of Japan's traditional religion, preaching that the greatest honour lay in sacrificing oneself for God-Emperor and nation. In 1933 Japan withdrew from the League of Nations and accelerated its armaments programmes. From bases in northeast China, Japan's Kwantung Army expanded to establish its own Chinese puppet-state, Manchukuo, and in 1937 marched into northern China. China's resistance was hampered by savage rivalry between the Nationalists led by Chiang Kai-shek and the Communists under Chu Teh and Mao Tse-tung. The Western powers condemned Japan's actions but at first did little to aid China.

Japanese pilots receive a briefing in 1939, when Japan's military machine had already moved against China. Some 'experts' then said Japan's planes were poor copies of Western types, and their pilots were physically unfit for combat. They were very wrong.

20

The 'tiger shark' markings on these P-40 Warhawks were first seen in the East in late 1941, when the 'Flying Tigers', U.S. pilots recruited to aid China, entered combat against the Japanese.

A Chinese soldier stands guard over U.S. warplanes. China's resistance to Japan was hampered by rivalry between Nationalists led by Chiang Kai-shek and Communists under Mao Tse-tung.

A priest bows to Emperor Hirohito, until 1945 a living god to the Japanese, as the ruler visits Tokyo's Yasukuni Shrine, sacred to Japan's military dead. The State Shinto religion helped prepare Japan for war.

❑ One of the worst atrocities of modern times was the 'Rape of Nanking', December 1937. Japanese troops who had taken the Chinese port (below) were allowed to run wild: some 50,000 civilians were murdered. American official protest centred on the sinking during air attacks on Nanking of the gunboat USS *Panay*.

❑ Japan, which in 1922 had operated the first true aircraft carrier, *Hosho* (beating the British *Hermes* by eight months), began to build the world's biggest battleships in 1936. The *Yamato* and *Musashi* displaced more than 70,000 tonnes full load (armour accounting for one-third of this tonnage), and each mounted nine 460mm (18.1in) guns. Both were sunk by U.S. air attack during World War II.

❑ Pilots of the American Volunteer Group ('Flying Tigers') were paid $750 per month, with a $500 bonus for every 'kill'. Between December 1941 and June 1942 they shot down 286 Japanese planes for only 23 losses.

Lightning war in Poland

In 1938 Germany forced Austria into union with her and occupied much of Czechoslovakia, drawing only weak protest from the western democracies. Concluding a non-aggression pact with Stalin's U.S.S.R. in August 1939, Hitler made his boldest move: the invasion of Poland. At dawn on September 1, 1939, five German armies, supported by c.1,700 aircraft, launched a *blitzkrieg* ('lightning war'). Surprise air attacks disrupted Polish airfields; then German planes struck supply routes and troop concentrations. Poland's armies, inferior in numbers (some 1 million men to Germany's 1.5 million) and equipment (Poland had 900 tanks; Germany more than 2,000), were battered by divebombers and had their lines pierced by rapid panzer (armoured) thrusts. German mechanized infantry swarmed into the gaps, securing passage for more tanks to drive into the Polish interior. The isolated Polish forward forces were encircled and mopped up by artillery and infantry. Britain and France declared war on Germany on September 3, but they could not help Poland. By September 15 the Germans had surrounded Warsaw; smashed apart by air and artillery bombardment, which killed c.40,000 citizens, the Polish capital surrendered on September 27. The conquest, which cost Germany only 43,000 casualties (203,000 Poles were killed or wounded; 694,000 captured) was completed on October 6. Meanwhile, Soviet forces occupied eastern Poland, taking 217,000 Polish prisoners (including 4,500 officers whom they would murder at Katyn Wood early in 1940).

The Polish eagle is ruthlessly tumbled from its perch as jubilant German infantrymen sweep aside the border barrier.

The triumphal march of German troops features the stiff-legged 'goose step', their ceremonial pace.

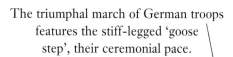

German armies hit Poland from three sides: from East Prussia in the north, Germany in the west, Czechoslovakia in the south. The U.S.S.R. took eastern Poland (green area).

U.S.S.R.

Danzig

GERMANY

Warsaw

POLAND

Prague

CZECH

AUSTRIA

Soviet forces moved into eastern Poland from September 17, 1939. Here, Red Army combat engineers use pontoons to replace a river bridge destroyed by the retreating Polish army.

Hitler takes the salute at a victory parade in Warsaw. Poland's capital was battered into surrender on September 27, 1939; on 19 October Hitler proclaimed west Poland part of the German *Reich* (empire).

❑ Germany claimed Poland had struck first, producing bodies of 'Polish soldiers' killed attacking a German border post at Gleiwitz on August 31. But the 'attack' was planned by S.S. deputy-leader Reinhard Heydrich, and the bodies were those of concentration camp inmates, dressed in Polish uniforms and murdered by the S.S.

❑ British writers J.F.C. Fuller and Basil Liddell Hart have been called the 'inventors' of *blitzkrieg*. But the tactics were pioneered by German General Oskar von Hutier in 1917-18, and perfected by General Heinz Guderian, who led an armoured corps in the Polish campaign.

❑ The German word for tank is *Panzerkampfwagen* (PzKw.; 'armoured fighting vehicle'), and German tanks are often called 'panzers'. Of more than 2,000 panzers committed to the Polish campaign, some 1,600 were PzKw.I or II (below), lightly armoured tanks of 5.5 tonnes and 9.5 tonnes respectively, their heaviest weapon a 20mm gun. But they outweighed the 2.5 tonne 'tankettes' of Polish units.

The 'Winter War'

In spite of their non-aggression pact, the U.S.S.R. did not trust Germany, and began to strengthen her frontiers. In October 1939 she demanded territorial concessions from Finland, whose eastern border lay within a few kilometres of Leningrad and the vital northern port of Murmansk. The Finns refused. On November 30, Russian planes bombed the Finnish capital Helsinki and four armies (c.600,000 men) attacked along the frontier. The Finns were outnumbered about three to one in men and were far inferior in warplanes and armour. But the Red Army had been demoralized by Stalin's 'purge' of officers, and it was ill-equipped for warfare in arctic conditions. Russian mechanized units bogged down in deep snow; Finnish 'commandos' raced in on skis to cut up isolated detachments. Thousands of Russians died in badly planned attacks on the 'Mannerheim Line', the Finnish emplacements across the Karelian Isthmus, north of Leningrad. At Suomussalmi in the central sector, on December 11-January 9, two Russian divisions were wiped out by Finnish ambush and encirclement tactics, losing 28,000 men at a cost of only 900 Finnish dead. But Anglo-French plans to send volunteers to aid Finland, never very realistic, were frustrated by Scandinavian neutrality, and at last sheer weight of numbers triumphed. With ruthless Marshal Timoshenko in command, Soviet 'human wave' attacks breached the Mannerheim Line. The Finns were forced to accept peace terms, ceding the territories demanded, on March 12, 1940. The Russians had lost some 200,000 dead (many from cold); the Finns only 25,000. In June 1941, Finland joined Germany in attacking the U.S.S.R.

Soviet armies struck all along Finland's eastern border. Fiercest fighting was in the central forests, lakes and swamps, and on the Mannerheim Line in the Karelian Isthmus, north of Leningrad (St. Petersburg).

Marshal Semyon Timoshenko (1895-1970), seen here (left) during pre-war manoeuvres, directed the assault on the Mannerheim Line.

The Finns had many highly trained ski troops like these, while the Soviets relied on motorized transport. When Russian trucks and armour bogged down in snow, fast moving Finnish commando units ambushed them and inflicted very heavy losses.

Tough concrete bunkers studded the Mannerheim Line, the Finnish defence works planned by and named after their leader, Marshal Baron Karl von Mannerheim (1867-1951).

Lacking heavy guns, the Finns were driven from their bunkers by long range fire directed by Soviet artillery observers, as seen here.

White coveralls camouflage the packs of Finnish ski troops, who often used reindeer as draught animals.

FACT FILE

❏ The 'Winter War' added the 'Molotov Cocktail' to the international armoury. The Finns mockingly called their improvised anti-tank grenade – a petrol-filled bottle with a rag wick – after the Soviet Foreign Minister, Vyacheslav Molotov (1890-1986) (above). They named the incendiary cluster-bombs dropped by Soviet planes 'Molotov Breadbaskets'.

❏ Finland had a handful of tanks; Russia more than 1,000 (of which some 300 were destroyed). In the breakthrough on the Mannerheim Line in February 1940, the Soviets combat-tested new 'giant' tanks: the 45 tonne SMK and 56 tonne T-100, experimental tanks with two turrets, and the 47 tonne KV-1, which would serve throughout World War II. Another combat 'first' was the Soviet use (on only a small scale) of paratroopers. The Red Army had experimented with paratroopers from 1930, and had formed its first airborne assault regiment as early as 1934-35.

Onslaught in the west

From September 1939, France awaited German attack. A British Expeditionary Force (B.E.F.) deployed against a German thrust through Belgium, while near the German frontier some 400,000 Frenchmen garrisoned the forts of the Maginot Line. On April 9, 1940, to secure access to Swedish iron ore, Germany invaded Norway and Denmark. Denmark fell in one day; Norway, aided by Anglo-French forces, held out until June 8. By then, Hitler had launched his western offensive. On May 10, spearheaded by parachute and glider troops who seized bridges and strongpoints, *blitzkrieg* hit Belgium (where fighting continued until May 27) and Holland (which surrendered on May 14, after air attack had devastated the city of Rotterdam). On May 12, in a bold move planned by General Fritz von Manstein, Germany's main armoured thrust was made through the supposedly 'untankable' Ardennes Forest, outflanking the Maginot Line. On paper, the opponents were evenly matched; each had 136 divisions and up to 3,000 tanks. But Germany had some 3,000 planes to the Allies' 1,800, and her forces were better trained, better organized and better commanded. German tanks raced to the Channel coast, cutting in two the Anglo-French forces. A 'panzer pause' on May 24-26 gave the Allies time to organize 'Operation Dynamo', the evacuation of c.338,000 British and French troops from the Channel port of Dunkirk. Italy declared war as Germany's ally on June 10, and invaded southern France on June 20. By June 25, French resistance ended. Hitler was master of western Europe; Britain stood alone against Germany.

Germany's attack on Western Europe began with occupation of Denmark on April 9, 1940. Norway fell on June 8; Holland on May 14; Belgium on May 27. France fell in June, but Allied troops escaped from Dunkirk.

'Cleopatra's Needle', a famous Parisian landmark, witnesses the entry of German invaders into France's capital on June 14, 1940.

German motorized infantrymen rumble through the streets of Paris in a half-tracked armoured personnel carrier. The city would remain under German occupation until its liberation in August 1944.

French *poilus* and a British 'tommy' (centre) celebrate the New Year of 1940 in the Maginot Line, a chain of fortresses on France's eastern border. By striking through the Ardennes, a forested area thought impenetrable by tanks, German armoured columns outflanked the Maginot Line.

Allied soldiers crowd the deck of a ship deployed in 'Operation Dynamo'. On May 26-June 4, 1940, an armada of small craft ferried many thousand troops from the beaches of Dunkirk to safety in England.

King Leopold III of Belgium (1901-83) personally commanded his nation's brief but brave resistance in 1940.

❏ There was so little action on the Western Front in September 1939-April 1940 that an American journalist named the period 'the Phoney War'. The Germans called it the *Sitzkrieg*.

❏ A major factor in Germany's victory was her 'flying artillery': Junkers Ju 87 'Stuka' divebombers (below). The Stuka delivered its bombs with great accuracy, breaking up obstacles to the armoured advance. Hurtling down with wing-mounted sirens shrieking, it demoralized those troops that it did not destroy.

❏ Close communication between air and ground forces was vital to the success of *blitzkrieg*, and German field communications were superior to Allied methods in 1940-41. The Germans relied heavily on the 'Enigma' cipher machine. From 1940 its codes were broken by the British, giving rise to the vital 'Ultra' intelligence system.

The 'Sealion' and the 'Eagle'

'The Battle of France is over . . . the Battle of Britain is about to begin', said British premier Winston Churchill on June 18, 1940. On July 16, Hitler issued orders for 'Operation Sealion', the invasion of Britain. An armada of c.2, 500 landing craft, to carry 20 divisions to southern England, began to assemble in the Channel ports. Its commanders insisted that no invasion could be made until Germany, inferior in naval strength in the Channel, had at least gained air supremacy. For the aerial 'Battle of Britain', the decisive phase of which began on *Adlertag* ('Eagle Day'), August 13, the Luftwaffe deployed c.2,500 combat aircraft. Britain had only 700-800 fighter planes at readiness, but was building 300-500 per month. The British had the advantages of a chain of early-warning radar stations; of information on German movements gained by 'Ultra' code-breaking; and of fighting in their own air space, so many 'downed' pilots quickly returned to combat. The agility of the R.A.F.'s Spitfire fighter gave it an edge on the German Messerschmitt Bf 109; the durable Hurricane, backbone of the defence, took heavy toll of German medium bombers. By September 15, the Luftwaffe had lost some 1,880 planes and 2,660 aircrew; R.A.F. Fighter Command had lost 1,020 planes and 537 pilots. If German bombers had concentrated on radar stations and airfields, rather than switching to London early in September, the R.A.F. might have been defeated. As it was, Hitler abandoned all plans for 'Sealion' in mid-October.

Taking office as Britain's war leader at a most perilous time, May 1940, Winston Churchill (1874-1965) told his people: 'I have nothing to offer but blood, toil, tears and sweat.'

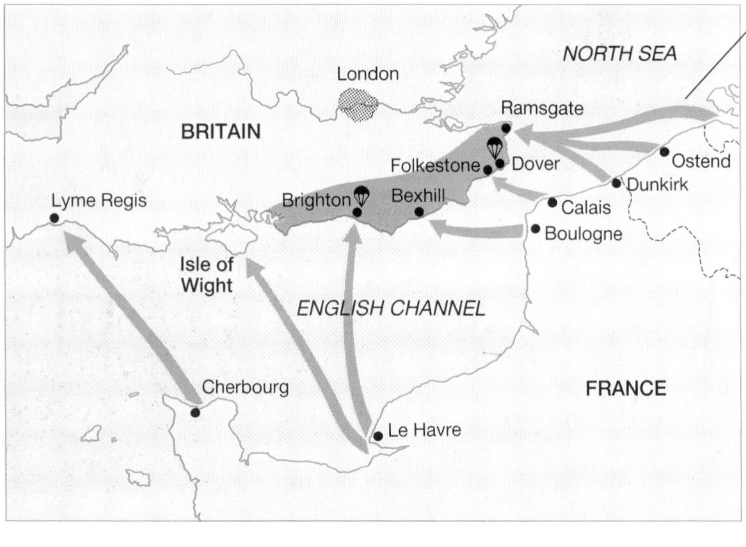

The German plan for 'Operation Sealion', the invasion of Britain ordered by Hitler in July 1940. Paratroop landings at Dover and Brighton, and a diversionary attack at Lyme Regis, would soften up the defenders and prepare for major seaborne landings. These would establish a bridgehead (shaded area) along England's southeast coast.

The Supermarine Spitfire proved a thoroughbred of air combat in the 'Battle of Britain'. It was fast (the Mark I's top speed was c.580kmh/360mph); agile and hard hitting, with an armament of eight 0.303in machine guns.

Map labels: NORTH SEA, London, BRITAIN, Ramsgate, Folkestone, Dover, Ostend, Brighton, Bexhill, Dunkirk, Lyme Regis, Calais, Boulogne, Isle of Wight, ENGLISH CHANNEL, Cherbourg, FRANCE, Le Havre

Air warfare was a grim business – but many flyers added a light touch by having personal emblems on their planes. This pilot favoured 'Donald Duck' as a mascot.

Britain's fight back was aided by Europeans who had fled German occupation of their homelands, like these Polish pilots serving with the R.A.F.

FACT FILE

❑ The Royal Navy had suffered heavy loss during the Dunkirk evacuation. The U.S.A., although neutral, came to Britain's aid. On August 13, 1940, under a 'lend-lease' agreement, President Roosevelt handed over 50 old U.S.N. destroyers in exchange for leases on naval bases in the Caribbean.

❑ Winston Churchill became Britain's war leader, heading a coalition (all-party) government, on May 10, 1940. Born of an American mother, he was described as 'half American – and all English'.

❑ In 1940 the top secret 'Coats Mission' was formed. Lieutenant Colonel J.S. Coats commanded a company of Guardsmen (with civilian buses for transport) and four armoured cars. His task, if the Germans landed, was to whisk the British Royal family to a place of safety.

❑ Churchill paid unforgettable tribute to the R.A.F.'s fighter pilots (below) on August 20, 1940: 'Never in the field of human conflict was so much owed by so many to so few.'

Rain of terror

Before and during World War II, some experts on air warfare believed that 'area bombing', devastating attacks on enemy cities to break the morale of their people, could win a war. From September 1940, Hitler tested this theory. Infuriated by the R.A.F.'s first night raid on Berlin, August 25-26, he ordered massive raids on London. Between September 7-November 12, the British capital suffered 58 major attacks: some 15,000 civilians were killed and more than 250,000 'bombed out' (made homeless). Then the night raids were extended to other cities. In the most destructive, on November 14-15, 449 bombers destroyed about one-third of the historic city of Coventry. The 'Blitz' went on until May 1941 – when the German bomber force withdrew to prepare for the imminent attack on the U.S.S.R. More than 40,000 civilians were killed and some 86,000 seriously injured. The Luftwaffe had few heavy bombers, and the payloads of such twin-engined planes as the Heinkel He 111, Dornier Do 17 and Junkers Ju 88 were small. More harm was done by incendiary (fire-raising) bombs – more than 2 million buildings were destroyed or damaged – than by high explosive. But at a cost of more than 600 bombers, the Luftwaffe failed seriously to damage Britain's war industries, or to break the spirit of her people. There were some incidents of panic and looting, but most civilians justified the slogan: 'Britain can take it!' Meanwhile the R.A.F. prepared for its own bombing campaign: its first four-engined, heavy bomber, the Short Stirling, became operational on February 10, 1941.

Throughout the war, Britain's army of volunteer Civil Defence workers stood ready to face the air raid peril.

Remains of a German night raider lie in a battered suburban street in southeast England, major target of the Blitz.

A gas mask in a slung haversack and a steel helmet are essential equipment for a C.D. worker.

From early 1941 the R.A.F. hit back at Germany with its first four-engined, heavy bomber, the Short Stirling.

The Luftwaffe's swastika emblem remains faintly visible on the wreck's tail.

Action stations

Since the days of sail, the big guns of the 'ship of the line' had dominated sea warfare – and the first major sea battle of World War II was a traditional gunnery action. On December 13, 1939, the German 'pocket battleship' (a heavy cruiser, with six 279mm/11in guns) *Admiral Graf Spee* was intercepted off the River Plate, Uruguay, by three smaller British cruisers. Outgunned but more agile, the British ships attacked from two sides, forcing the damaged *Spee* to take refuge in neutral Montevideo. Bluffed into believing the British had brought up reinforcements, *Spee*'s captain scuttled his ship on December 17. Soon, however, the aircraft and submarine showed the new shape of sea warfare. On November 11-12, 1940, 12 British Swordfish torpedo biplanes from the aircraft carrier *Illustrious* crippled three Italian battleships in a daring night attack on Taranto harbour. Air power was also instrumental in the sinking of the German 'supership' *Bismarck* (42,000 tonnes; eight 381mm/15in guns). On May 18, 1941, *Bismarck* sortied into the Atlantic, and on May 24, in a long-range gunnery action, sank the British battle cruiser *Hood* (only 3 of her 1,400 crewmen surviving). In the ensuing sea chase, torpedo hits by Swordfish from the carrier *Ark Royal* crippled *Bismarck*'s steering, enabling British battleships and cruisers to batter her into a flaming wreck on May 27. But meanwhile German submarines threatened to cut Britain's supply lines: by December 1939, U-boats had sunk 114 ships, compared to 79 sunk by mines and only 15 by surface action.

British submariners prepare for action, 1940. As in World War I, submarines had a major role.

The reliable 533mm (21in) Mark VIII torpedo was the main armament of the Royal Navy's submarines.

Captain Hans Langsdorff, commanding officer of *Admiral Graf Spee*, committed suicide three days after his ship's destruction.

The end of a German 'pocket battleship'. After a mauling by British cruisers off the coast of Uruguay, *Admiral Graf Spee* is blown up by her own crew outside Montevideo harbour late on December 17, 1939.

The Fairey Swordfish torpedo biplane ('Stringbag' to its crews) that equipped British aircraft carriers early in the war was slow (with a top speed of c.225kmh/ 140mph), but often proved its worth in combat.

The 22,000 tonne *Ark Royal* was the Royal Navy's only modern aircraft carrier in 1939. Many times 'sunk' by German propaganda, the 'Old Ark' was finally lost after being hit by a torpedo from a German submarine late in 1941.

FACT FILE

❏ Unrevealed until the 1970s was the part played by U.S. forces in the destruction of the *Bismarck*. After British ships lost contact, *Bismarck* was sighted by a U.S.C.G. cutter and shadowed by a PBY Catalina seaplane (on loan to Britain, but with a U.S.N. pilot) which aided *Ark Royal*'s Swordfish to locate the battleship.

❏ When France fell, Britain feared Germany would take over powerful French warships. So on July 4, 1940, British ships bombarded the French naval base at Mers-el-Kébir, Algeria, sinking the battleship *Bretagne* and killing more than 1,000 French sailors.

❏ The first U.S. warship sunk in World War II was the destroyer *Reuben James*, torpedoed by a U-boat off Iceland, October 31, 1939, with the loss of more than 100 lives. After 1941, the U.S.N. was the only service of World War II to use airships: its 76m (250ft) long 'blimps' (below), crewed by 9-12 men and with a top speed of c.121kmh (75mph) and a range of 3,218km (2,000mi), made anti-submarine patrols off the U.S. coastline.

'Desert Rats' versus the 'Desert Fox'

Italy entered World War II on June 10, 1940. Her main threat to Britain was in North Africa. Superior in men (c.250,000 to 70,000 British and Commonwealth troops), armour and planes, the Italians advanced from their colony of Libya into Egypt, towards the Suez Canal, on September 13, 1940. But Italian morale was poor – many Italians had not wanted war – and after a brief and costly advance they halted in 10 fortified 'camps'. When British General Wavell launched a counteroffensive in November-December the Italians retreated swiftly and tens of thousands surrendered. The British took the vital Libyan supply port of Tobruk on January 22, 1941, and on February 6-7, under General Richard O'Connor, won their first great land victory of the war, destroying the Italian 10th Army (25,000 prisoners; only 50 British casualties) at Beda Fomm. But now Hitler dispatched the German *Afrika Korps* under General Rommel to the aid of the Italians. Rommel's orders were only to block the British advance – but instead he launched his smaller force into offensives characterized by speed, surprise and improvisation (as when the German 88mm anti-aircraft gun proved a battle-winning anti-tank weapon). Weakened by the removal of veteran troops to Greece (invaded by Italy in October 1940 and by Germany in April 1941), Wavell was soon driven back into Egypt. Rommel besieged Tobruk: its capture, in June 1942, won him promotion to Field Marshal; the disastrous failure of British attempts to relieve it cost Wavell his command.

Field Marshal Erwin Rommel (1891-1944) was one of Germany's best commanders. Here he wears the Knight's Cross and (lower) the *Pour le Mérite*, Germany's highest award for valour during World War I.

Medium tanks of an Axis armoured formation navigate a sea of sand in the Western Desert, c.1941. Much of the terrain was like a featureless ocean, where 'fleets' of tanks cruised like warships at sea.

Desert warfare involved tricky supply problems. Sand penetrated and wore out tank engines; lack of petrol or water crippled an armoured force as surely as shellfire.

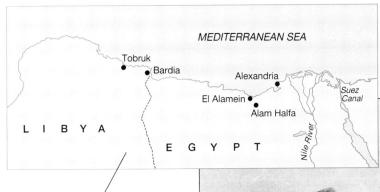

The map locates major sites in the North African campaign of 1940-42 (see also *pages 54-55*). The Italians, later supported by the German *Afrika Korps*, advanced from Libya towards the Suez Canal. Motorized armies clashed in a vast area of desert, scrub and marsh.

General Sir Alan Cunningham (1887-1984) drove Italian forces from East Africa, 1940-41; then briefly commanded British 8th Army in North Africa. Note the *topi* (sun hat) worn by the officer with him.

'Free French' forces, like these colonial troops from Senegal, fought alongside the Allies.

❏ One of the first victims of the Italian defenders of Tobruk was their own leader. Air Marshal Italo Balbo, commander-in-chief of Italian forces in North Africa, died when his plane was shot down by Italian A.A.A. on June 28, 1940. Because he had opposed Italy's entry into the war, it is said that this may not have been an 'accident'.

❏ British 7th Armoured Division won its nickname, 'Desert Rats', for its 'scurrying and biting' aggression under O'Connor in 1941. Its divisional sign, the jerboa rodent of the North African desert, was once again borne proudly into action in 1991, when it formed part of the Allied force in Operation 'Desert Storm', the liberation of Kuwait.

❏ Shrewd, audacious General Erwin Rommel was much respected, even liked, by his opponents, who named him the 'Desert Fox'. Churchill called him 'daring and skilful . . . a great general'. General Auchinleck (below), Wavell's successor, complained of 'a real danger that . . . Rommel is becoming a kind of magician or bogey-man to our troops'.

Fight for the Middle Sea

Italy's invasion of neutral Greece on October 28, 1940, was repulsed with heavy loss, but early in April 1941 Germany, Italy and Hungary launched 'Operation Marita' for the conquest of Yugoslavia, where an anti-Axis government had taken power, and Greece. Yugoslavia surrendered on April 17; Greece, after fierce resistance aided by the British 'W Force', on 28 April. 'W Force', less some 10,000 taken prisoner, was evacuated by the R.N. to the island of Crete. On 20 May, Hitler committed c.30,000 men to a predominantly airborne invasion of Crete. General Freyberg's British and Greek defenders, some 35,000 strong, had lost their heavy equipment in Greece, but at first took severe toll of German paratroopers and glider troops, while the R.N. prevented German reinforcement by sea. But the Germans had air superiority and, after capturing an airfield, were able to airlift in new troops, forcing Freyberg's surrender on June 1. Some 16,000 Allied troops were evacuated by sea; more than 18,000 became prisoners. Nevertheless, heavy German losses (c.7,000 paratroopers dead or wounded) helped persuade Hitler to abandon plans for an airborne invasion of Malta. The operations of British surface ships, submarines and planes from this island fortress against Rommel's Mediterranean supply lines were vital to victory in North Africa. From April 1941 to November 1942 Malta was under almost constant air attack, with c.3,000 air raids by up to 300 planes at a time. Aircraft for its defence were flown in from carriers; supplies were fought through in convoys suffering up to 80 per cent loss.

Yugoslavia fell after an 11-day *blitzkrieg*, April 6-17, 1941. Here, a German armoured column rolls into a Serbian town.

A Yugoslavian supply convoy has been destroyed – but Yugoslav guerrillas would later fight back fiercely.

Hitler poses with one of his paratroopers (*Fallschirmjäger*) in 1940, when daring raids by airborne troops spearheaded the German invasions of Scandinavia, Holland and Belgium.

Aircraft carriers (of which Britain then had few; but Germany and Italy had none) played a vital part in the defence of Malta, 1941-42.

Dropping from Junkers Ju 52 transport aircraft, German paratroopers descend on Crete in May 1941.

Paratroopers are ready for action as soon as they hit the ground. Many German airborne troops landed on Crete in gliders, which often crashed. Slower to deploy, they took heavier casualties.

Fighters are made ready aboard a British carrier. With Malta under almost permanent air attack, carriers ferried fighters through the Mediterranean to reinforce the island.

FACT FILE

❏ 'Ultra' intelligence told the British of German plans to invade Crete – and provoked a controversy that still rages. Some historians say General Freyberg misunderstood the warning and, thinking the main attack would be made by sea, deployed his troops badly. Others maintain that Freyberg was ordered not to deploy against an airborne onslaught, for fear the Germans might guess that their codes had been broken.

❏ One paratrooper who jumped on Crete was Max Schmeling, world heavyweight boxing champion in 1930-32. The Nazis had promoted him as an 'Aryan superman' when he fought the great U.S. black boxer Joe Louis. Schmeling detested this propaganda.

❏ The Maltese people survived constant air attack (below) by digging out huge shelters in the soft limestone rock of their small island. Their 'heroism and devotion' was recognized on April 16, 1942, by King George VI, who awarded to the island the George Cross, Britain's highest award for civilian gallantry.

'Barbarossa'

'General Winter', the ice and snow of Russia, stopped the German advance on Moscow – just as it has stalled this Volkswagen communications car.

Hitler said of his attack on the U.S.S.R.: 'We have only to kick in the door and the whole rotten structure will come crashing down.' His 'kick', a surprise attack called 'Operation Barbarossa', was launched on June 22, 1941. Three Army Groups – some 150 divisions (3,000,000-plus men), with some 4,000 tanks, 7,000 artillery pieces and c.3,000 aircraft – attacked along a 3,220km (2,000mi) front. The Soviets had more than 3,000,000 men, up to 7,000 aircraft and c.20,000 tanks, but much of their equipment was outdated. The Red Air Force was caught on the ground, losing more than 1,000 planes on the first day. *Blitzkrieg* advance trapped huge Russian armies in 'pockets': 500,000 were captured in the Minsk 'pocket' and 300,000 in the Bialystok 'pocket' in June; 300,000 in the Smolensk 'pocket' in July. But by then the Germans had taken 450,000 casualties. Late in August, Hitler changed his original plan – a major effort to take Moscow and the U.S.S.R.'s industrial heartland – and diverted strong forces to encircle 700,000 Russians in the Kiev 'pocket'. Not until November did he order the final drive on Moscow, and by then winter had set in. Early in December, only 32km (20mi) from Moscow, whose fall might have broken Russia's will to resist, Field Marshal von Bock's armour literally froze to a halt. The Russians had been given time to rally in defence of their capital – and to move vital war industries from the Moscow region to havens east of the Ural Mountains, where they were safe from attack by an air force lacking long-ranged, heavy bombers.

Field Marshal Fedor von Bock (1880-1945) commanded German Army Group Centre in the drive on the Soviet capital, Moscow, in 1941.

With sabres drawn, Cossack cavalrymen lead machine gun carts into action. Almost certainly a posed Soviet propaganda photograph – but a most impressive sight.

When motor vehicles froze to a standstill, traditional transport, like this horse drawn sledge, was used.

This German observer is well wrapped against the cold – but many Germans were without winter gear and froze to death on the East Front.

❏ Hitler codenamed his attack in honour of Emperor Frederick I Barbarossa ('Red Beard') (c.1123-90), one of the strongest war leaders of the Middle Ages. In legend, Barbarossa lies sleeping until Germany needs his aid.

❏ Stalin was warned of German invasion plans by British 'Ultra' intelligence, passed on through the German-Swiss 'Lucy' spy ring, and by Richard Sorge (1895-1944), Germany's top spy in Tokyo – in fact, a Soviet double agent (arrested by the Japanese later in 1941; executed in 1944). The Soviet dictator, for reasons which remain unclear, failed to take full advantage of the warnings.

❏ 'On paper' German-Soviet tank strengths for 'Barbarossa' are misleading. Only about 2,000 German tanks were modern PzKw.III and IV models; the Russians had about the same number of up to date KV-1, KV-2 and T-34 models.

❏ In parts of the Ukraine and elsewhere, the invading Germans were welcomed as liberators from Communist tyranny. But the German policy of treating Slavic peoples as *Untermenschen* (sub-human slave races) alienated many potential collaborators and allowed Stalin (whom history now sees as a tyrant equal to Hitler) to rally support for what Russian historians call 'The Great Patriotic War'.

Pearl Harbor: day of infamy

By late 1941 Western economic sanctions had cut off some 90 per cent of Japan's oil supplies. Japan saw the conquest of Pacific territories rich in raw materials as her only path to survival. As a first step, Admiral Isoroku Yamamoto planned the destruction of the U.S. Pacific Fleet. On November 26, 1941, Admiral Chuichi Nagumo's task force, with six aircraft carriers, began the 5,470km (3,400mi) voyage from Japan to Hawaii. At dawn on December 7, c.420km (260mi) north of Oahu Island, it began to launch its 360 aircraft. In the U.S. naval base at Pearl Harbor, Oahu, about 100 warships lay at anchor; c.500 warplanes stood in neat rows on airfields (where nearly 200 would be destroyed). Japan's first strike, by 183 torpedo planes and divebombers at 0750 hours, achieved complete surprise; a second strike by 170 aircraft followed. Within two hours, four of the Pacific Fleet's nine battleships were sunk (along with three light cruisers, three destroyers, and smaller craft) and four seriously damaged. Some 2,500 Americans died – 1,177 of them in the explosion of the battleship *Arizona*. The Japanese lost 29 aircraft. But Nagumo failed to catch the Pacific Fleet's three aircraft carriers (all were at sea) and, equally importantly, did not destroy Pearl Harbor's oil storage and repair facilities, thus allowing the U.S.N. to make a quick recovery. Japan's declaration of war was made immediately after Pearl Harbor (according to Japan, accident prevented its delivery immediately before), which President Roosevelt called 'a day that will live in infamy'.

A fiery pall wraps the U.S. battleship *West Virgina*, struck by seven torpedoes. Sunk in shallow water, she was raised and was back in service in 1944.

Hit by an armour piercing bomb, the powder magazine of the battleship *Arizona* explodes, killing more than 1,000 sailors.

Lying next to *West Virginia* in 'Battleship Row', off Ford Island, U.S.S. *Tennessee*, in the inshore berth, took two bomb hits without serious damage. She was ready for action within a few weeks.

Braving flaming debris, a motor launch moves in to pluck men from the water alongside the *West Virginia*. Damage done by the surprise attack was less than the Japanese hoped.

This map, which serves also as a locator for the campaigns described on *pages 42-51*, shows the vast area that lay under Japan's control by mid-1942. It included much of China, Southeast Asia and the western Pacific. —

CHINA

JAPAN

PACIFIC OCEAN

Midway Island

Wake Island

Hawaiian Is.
Pearl Harbor

Hong Kong

Marianas Islands

Philippine Islands

Marshall Islands

Singapore

Gilbert Islands

Papua-New Guinea

Guadalcanal

AUSTRALIA

Japanese Empire perimeter, 1941-42

❏ U.S. cryptanalysts 'broke' Japan's top diplomatic and military codes in September 1941, giving rise to the vital 'Magic' intelligence system (the British equivalent was 'Ultra'). 'Magic' warned that Japan would strike in December 1941 – but was unable to say where, because Nagumo's task force kept total radio silence.

❏ Early on December 7, Japanese fleet submarines launched five midget submarines (below) that were intended to penetrate Pearl Harbour. All five were lost, the first at 0645 hours – one hour before the first air strike – when the destroyer USS *Ward* sank it at the harbor entrance.

❏ Admiral Husband E. Kimmel (1882-1968) and General Walter C. Short (1880-1949), respectively U.S. naval and army commanders at Pearl Harbor, were charged with 'dereliction of duty', and both retired from service in 1942.

'Battling Bastards'

On December 8, 1941, the U.S.A. and Britain declared war on Japan; Germany and Italy declared war on the U.S.A. on December 11. By then Japan had attacked the Philippine Islands, defended by General Douglas MacArthur, commanding U.S. Army Forces in the Far East, with some 120,000 troops (including c.35,000 Americans). A few hours after Pearl Harbor, Japanese planes from Formosa (Taiwan) hit MacArthur's airfields, destroying most of his planes on the ground. On December 22, General Homma's 14th Army (c.50,000 men) landed at Lingayen Gulf, c.240km (150mi) north of Manila; another strong Japanese force landed southeast of Manila on December 24. MacArthur made a skilful, fighting retreat to prepared defence lines on the Bataan peninsula, where he hoped to hold out until reinforced. Although short of food and medical supplies, MacArthur's troops inflicted heavy casualties (c.12,000 throughout the campaign) on the Japanese, but Japan's control of air and sea prevented reinforcement. On March 11, 1942, MacArthur (vowing 'I shall return!') was ordered to leave for Australia, to become Supreme Commander South West Pacific. General Jonathan Wainwright fought on, but early in April the Japanese broke through. With 25,000 men sick, the 'Battling Bastards of Bataan' (' . . . no father, no mother – and no Uncle Sam'; i.e. no reinforcement) had to surrender on April 9. Wainwright, with c.15,000 men, made a last stand on the fortress island of Corregidor, surrendering on May 6, when water supplies were near exhausted.

The Japanese had planned to conquer the islands in two months, but took five.

Lieutenant General Masaharu Homma, commander of Japanese 14th Army, steps ashore at Luzon.

Heroic U.S. and Filipino resistance delayed the conquest in the Philippines far beyond Homma's estimate.

U.S. and Filipino prisoners carry wounded and sick comrades in improvised litters during their 96km (60mi) 'Death March' north from Bataan.

General Douglas MacArthur, U.S. commander in the Philippines, was ordered to escape before the islands fell. He promised: 'I shall return.'

Victorious Japanese soldiers lower the Stars and Stripes at Fort Mills, U.S. headquarters on the fortress island of Corregidor, which was starved into surrender on May 6, 1942.

FACT FILE

❏ Only one member of the U.S. House of Representatives voted against the declaration of war on December 8: Jeanette Rankin (Republican, Montana). Ms. Rankin (1880-1973) had voted against the declaration of World War I in 1917 – and in the 1960s opposed the Vietnam War.

❏ Of 75,000 prisoners – including 63,000 Filipinos – taken by the Japanese on Bataan, some 16,000 died of ill-treatment during a 96km (60mi) 'Death March' to a prison camp. Of 12,000 Americans captured, only about one third survived at the end of the war.

❏ Corregidor's pre-World War I fortifications dominated Manila harbour. Its heavy guns included four Model 1890 305mm (12in) mortars. Strongest point was Fort Drum, an islet completely encased in concrete up to 11m (36ft) thick, mounting four 356mm (14in) and four 152mm (6in) guns. When U.S. forces retook Corregidor in 1945, Army engineers had to pour in petrol to burn out Japanese in this 'concrete battleship'.

❏ Lieutenant General Masaharu Homma (1887-1946) lost his command for his delay in securing the Philippines and the heavy losses incurred in the campaign. In 1946 he was tried in Manila for war crimes, notably the Bataan 'Death March', found guilty, and executed by firing squad.

The greatest disaster

Malaya's tin and rubber were vital to Japan. On December 8, 1941, General Yamashita's 25th Army (c.40,000 men) landed in Siam (Thailand) – Japan's forced ally from December 14 – and northeast Malaya. The British battleships *Prince of Wales* and *Repulse* steamed to attack his bridgeheads. Without air cover, they were intercepted and sunk (840 dead) on December 10 by 90 Japanese bombers and torpedo planes (4 lost). Defending Malaya and the naval base of Singapore at its southern tip, Lieutenant General Arthur Percival had c.107,000 British and Commonwealth troops. Yamashita was outnumbered by more than two to one throughout the campaign, but he had 200 light tanks and 500 aircraft; Percival had no tanks, few anti-tank weapons and only 150 planes. The British blocked the highways, but Yamashita's jungle-trained infantry (often using bicycles) bypassed the roadblocks, leaving them to be mopped up by tanks. British defence lines were outflanked by amphibious landings along the east coast by 'marines' of the elite Imperial Guards Division. On January 30-31, 1942, Percival withdrew to Singapore Island, blowing up the causeway that joined it to the mainland. His defence was inept and his men's morale crumbled. On February 15, after the loss of the island's water reservoirs, Percival surrendered. Both sides suffered c.9,000 casualties; 130,000 British and Commonwealth troops became prisoners. In what Churchill called 'the greatest disaster in the history of the British Empire', Yamashita took Malaya and Singapore in 70 days rather than the 100 planned.

British and Commonwealth soldiers raised their hands in surrender when Singapore, the British Empire's 'eastern bulwark', fell on February 15, 1942.

Australian soldiers deploy a 25-pounder Mark II field gun against the Japanese advance in Malaya.

With bayonet fixed, a Japanese infantryman guards the captives. Many of them would fail to survive the years of harsh treatment to come.

General Tomoyuki Yamashita – victor in Malaya.

A staff officer in tropical 'whites' accompanies General Yamashita as the 'Tiger of Malaya' takes a walk through the ruined streets of Singapore.

❑ It is often said that Singapore fell because its big guns (above) 'pointed the wrong way', out to sea. In fact, its 381mm (15in) batteries could and did fire northward – but because of pre-war economies they had only armour-piercing ammunition, of little use against troop concentrations. The same economies had starved Singapore of modern warplanes and properly trained troops. Bad generalship, by Percival, Air Chief Marshal Sir Robert Brooke-Popham and others, did the rest.

❑ The Japanese captured some 45,000 men of Britain's Indian Army in Malaya. Many later joined the 'Indian National Army', raised by Subhas Chandra Bose (1897-1945), a fanatical foe of British rule, to support the Japanese invasion of India in 1944. Most claimed that they had intended to desert as soon as they re-entered India.

❑ The 35,000 tonne *Prince of Wales* was Britain's fastest, most modern battleship, only completed early in 1941.

Turning point at Midway

Admiral Yamamoto believed Japan must wage a speedy war of conquest and then negotiate peace. He planned the strike on Pearl Harbor, saying: 'For six months I shall run wild; after that, I don't know.' Japanese warships smashed an Allied force in the Java Sea (February 27, 1942), and drove the British Eastern Fleet from its base at Ceylon (Sri Lanka) early in April. Then Yamamoto moved south to cut off Australia, sending two aircraft carriers into the Coral Sea to support an invasion of Port Moresby, New Guinea. Aided by 'Magic' intelligence, U.S. Admiral Fletcher's carriers *Yorktown* and *Lexington* engaged them on May 7-8. Coral Sea was the first naval battle fought solely by carrier aircraft. The Japanese sank *Lexington* and damaged *Yorktown*, but they had a carrier badly damaged, lost many planes, and were forced to turn back from Port Moresby. Yamamoto believed he now had carrier superiority (in fact, *Yorktown* was quickly repaired), and planned a decisive battle. He committed his total strength to an invasion of Midway atoll and a diversionary attack on the Aleutian Islands. 'Magic' aided Admiral Nimitz, commanding U.S. Pacific Fleet, to concentrate his air power (three fleet carriers, plus Midway-based planes) on Yamamoto's four fleet carriers. On June 4-5, early U.S. air attacks were beaten off with heavy loss, but later strikes caught Japanese aircraft re-arming on the flight decks. All four Japanese fleet carriers were sunk; c.280 aircraft (with irreplaceable veteran aircrews) were lost. The U.S.N. lost *Yorktown* and c.135 planes. Japan's march of conquest was ended.

Biplane aircraft of 1930s vintage are ranked on the carrier's flight deck in this fine pre-war photograph.

U.S.S. *Saratoga* and her sister ship *Lexington* were launched in 1925. The *Lexington* was torpedoed and sunk at Midway; *Saratoga* survived the war.

Sailors in training with a ship mounted anti-aircraft gun; in action, gun crews would wear fire-proof overalls.

Allied warships' heavy A.A.A. included the British 102mm (4in) gun seen here and the U.S. Navy's 127mm (5in) gun, both either singly or twin mounted.

The Douglas SBD Dauntless dive bomber, with a c.454kg (1,000lb) bomb load, was the U.S. carrier forces' major strike aircraft at the Coral Sea and Midway.

Green hell: Guadalcanal

After losing four carriers at Midway, Japan tried to establish an air base on Guadalcanal, Solomon Islands, and by mid-1942 had an airstrip guarded by c.2,000 men. On August 7, 12,000 U.S. Marines under General Alexander A. Vandegrift landed, quickly capturing the airstrip (Henderson Field; operational from August 20). But the U.S.N.'s defeat off Savo Island, August 8-9, left the Marines short of supplies and under naval and air bombardment. Japanese reinforcements landed on August 18, but their reckless attack was bloodily repulsed on the Tenaru River, August 21. After a U.S. naval victory in the Eastern Solomons, August 23-25, Japanese reinforcement relied on the 'Tokyo Express' (night convoys of fast transports). On land, the Japanese were again defeated at 'Bloody Ridge', September 12-14, but still had c.25,000 men to Vandegrift's 23,000. But an attack across the Matanikau River, October 23-26, cost 3,500 Japanese lives, and their air support was weakened by losses in the naval battle of Santa Cruz, October 25-26. General Hyakutake's final attack on Henderson Field failed on November 19-21, and 'Carlson's Raiders' decimated the Japanese in eastern Guadalcanal. Big Japanese troop convoys were broken up in naval actions on November 12-15. Strong U.S. Army forces relieved the Marines in December and forced the Japanese back to Cape Esperance, where c.13,000 survivors were evacuated in February 1943. Guadalcanal cost the Japanese c.25,000 dead (including some 9,000 who died of disease or starvation in the island's 'green hell' of malarial jungle and swamp). U.S. losses were c.1,500 dead and 4,800 wounded.

Thigh deep in a swamp, the 'point man' leads a U.S. Marine patrol in the Solomons. Tough terrain and tropical diseases abounded on Guadalcanal.

This Marine keeps his M1 Garand rifle at the ready, alert for ambush. Marines became expert jungle fighters on Guadalcanal.

Wreckage of warships and planes – like this Japanese Mitsubishi G4M medium bomber – strewed the seas off the Solomons.

The map serves as a locator for both the island of Guadalcanal and for major events of the Papua-New Guinea campaign (see *pages 50-51*).

Hollandia

DUTCH NEW GUINEA

N.E. NEW GUINEA

Lae

PAPUA

Kokoda

Buna

The Slot

Port Moresby

GUADALCANAL

Kokoda Trail

The 11m (36ft) long 'Higgins boat' – the U.S. 'landing craft, vehicle, personnel' (LCVP) – could carry up to 36 fully equipped troops to assault enemy held beaches.

❑ U.S. victory on Guadalcanal depended on preventing Japanese reinforcement by sea. The campaign saw seven major naval battles, in which each side lost 24 ships. So many warships and transports were sunk in the strait north of Guadalcanal that from late 1942 the Allies called it 'Ironbottom Sound'.

❑ Japanese naval successes off Guadalcanal and elsewhere owed much to the Type 93 torpedo, largest and fastest of the war. Powered by liquid oxygen, the 'Long Lance' carried a 500kg (1,100lb) warhead to a maximum range of 40km (44,000yd) at 66kmh (41mph). The U.S. Mark 15 torpedo had a 300kg (660lb) warhead and a range of 14km (15,200yd) at 50kmh (31mph). The full sized, 610mm (24in) diameter, 'Long Lance' was launched from deck tubes on cruisers and destroyers. A smaller, 533mm (21in), Type 95 oxygen torpedo was developed for use by submarines.

❑ 'Carlson's Raiders' (2nd Raider Battalion, U.S.M.C.) was a commando unit formed by Brigadier General Evans F. Carlson (1896-1947). He based his methods on those used by Chinese Communist guerrillas against the Japanese. The Raiders' motto (now a catchword) was 'Gung-ho!' (Chinese: 'Work together!'). In one 30-day patrol, they claimed 500 Japanese killed for only 17 U.S. dead.

Nightmare in New Guinea

Japan needed bases on the big island of Papua-New Guinea to defend its southern Pacific conquests and to threaten Australia. An invasion force heading for Port Moresby, southern Papua, was turned back by the U.S. Navy in the Coral Sea, May 1942, but in July the Japanese landed in force at Gona, northern Papua, and advanced overland towards Port Moresby. At first they were opposed by half-trained militia rushed from Australia; then battle hardened 'Diggers' from the Middle East and U.S. troops under General Eichelberger moved in. The battle ground, said a U.S. general, was 'nightmare country': choking heat, densely forested mountain and swamp, rough trails blocked by razor edged scrub, alive with disease-bearing insects. The Japanese advance down the Kokoda Trail, over the Owen Stanley Mountains, was halted only 48km (30mi) from Port Moresby. The Allies drove them back in vicious hand-to-hand battles between men racked by malaria and dysentery. Many Japanese starved to death; some survived by cannibalism. In December 1942-January 1943, the Allies took by storm the Japanese fortifications at Gona and Buna. At least 7,000 Japanese died in the Kokoda campaign; the Allies had c.8,500 battle casualties, many more from disease. The threat to Port Moresby was lifted, but the struggle for Papua-New Guinea went on. In spite of a steady build up of Allied air power, under U.S. General Kenney, and brilliantly coordinated amphibious and airborne attacks as the Allies drove westward in 1943, Papua-New Guinea was not secured until mid-1944.

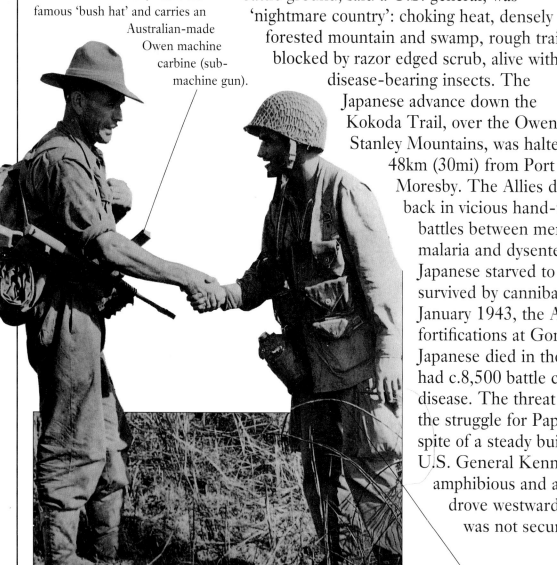

This 'Digger', as Australian soldiers were called, wears the famous 'bush hat' and carries an Australian-made Owen machine carbine (sub-machine gun).

The U.S. M4 Sherman tank was a battle winner in many theatres – but in New Guinea much terrain was 'untankable'.

A U.S. paratrooper greets his ally after joint operations by Australian ground troops and U.S. airborne forces have taken Japanese strongholds in northeast New Guinea, in late 1943.

The bow doors of a 'Landing Ship, Tank' (LST) gape wide as it prepares to load vehicles and men for a landing in New Guinea. Troops in combat gear march towards their embarkation points. American soldiers claimed that 'LST' meant 'Large, Slow Target'.

The bulldozer was a vital tool in jungle warfare, often used to clear away trees and level ground to build airstrips.

M3 light tanks lead the way for infantrymen as U.S. forces advance through the ruins of a Japanese position on New Britain, off New Guinea, in March 1944.

The jungle gave defenders good cover, and material for strong points like this Japanese bunker of coconut palm logs.

FACT FILE

❑ General MacArthur's frequent complaints over delay in securing Papua-New Guinea were unjust to three of the best commanders of the Pacific War. Australian General Sir Thomas Blamey (1884-1951) inspired his 'Diggers' on the Kokoda Trail, and then served loyally under the equally able U.S. General Robert L. Eichelberger (1886-1961) (above). Neither could have succeeded without General George C. Kenney (1889-1977), a genius of tactical air operations as commander of U.S. 5th Air Force. In 1950, Blamey was the first Australian soldier to be appointed Field Marshal.

❑ As the Japanese retreated on the Kokoda Trail, they left behind 'suicide snipers', tied into treetops. Later in the Pacific War, the U.S.M.C. formed 'K-9' units, using Dobermann Pinscher dogs to 'sniff out' hidden marksmen.

Wolves of the Atlantic

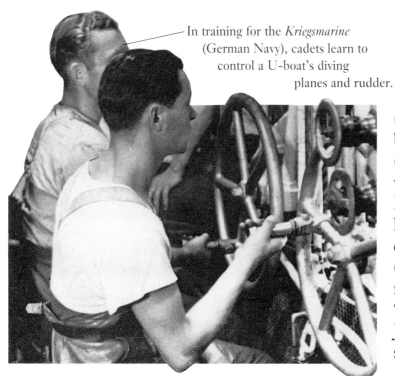

In training for the *Kriegsmarine* (German Navy), cadets learn to control a U-boat's diving planes and rudder.

The war's longest battle was fought on the Atlantic convoy routes between the U.S.A. and Britain. In September 1939, Admiral Dönitz, Germany's U-boat (*Unterseeboot*: submarine) commander, had only 57 boats, but by mid-1940 many more were in service (1,162 were built in 1939-45) and victory in the west had secured bases along the Atlantic coast. Dönitz ordered 'wolf pack' tactics: instead of hunting alone, all U-boats within range closed on a convoy, attacking by night and on the surface (where they could match the speed of most merchantmen). In their 'happy time', c.June 1940-June 1941, they sank 653 ships (c.2,788,000 tonnes).

Merchant ships steamed in 'convoy' groups like this so that they could be more easily protected by warship escorts.

An increased number of convoy escort warships, with improved sonar (sound detection) gear and surface radar, cut the loss rate – but another 'happy time' came when the U.S.A. was slow to adopt the convoy system. Up to mid-1942, 'Operation *Paukenschlag*' ('Drumbeat') sank several hundred ships, many just off the U.S. coasts. From 1943 the Allies closed the 'Black Gap' – the mid-ocean area out of range of land based aircraft – with the long ranged B-24 Liberator bomber and with small, mass produced aircraft carriers. Escort warships used 'Hedgehog' and 'Squid' mortars to throw 'patterns' of depthcharges on to submerged U-boats. Of 784 U-boats lost, 575 were sunk after May 1943. 'Super-boats', with improved engines and 'snorkel' breathing gear enabling them to run submerged at high speeds and for long periods, came too late to turn the tide. But the U-boats came close to cutting the Atlantic lifeline, sinking 2,828 ships (c.14,690,000 tonnes) in 1939-45.

A German U-boat returns from a war cruise in 1939. Germany entered the war with only 57 submarines, but had built more than 1,000 by 1945.

The conning tower of a surfaced U-boat was manned by the officer of the deck and by lookouts.

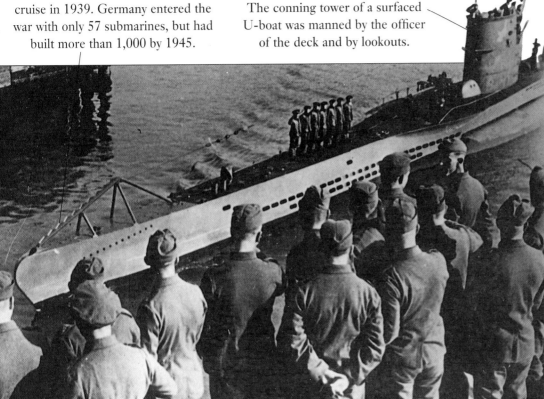

❏ Many cargo ships lost to U-boats were swiftly replaced thanks to U.S. industrialist Henry Kaiser (1882-1967). He developed welding techniques and assembly-line methods which made possible the completion of a 7,000-tonne merchant ship (above) within one month. The first of these 'Liberty' ships, *Patrick Henry*, was launched at Baltimore in September 1941; 2,770 were built during the war.

❏ Germany's U-boat 'ace' was Commander 'Silent Otto' Kretschmer (b.1912), who sank 44 merchantmen (c.267,000 tonnes) and a destroyer before his *U-99* was sunk in March 1941. As a prisoner in Britain and Canada, Kretschmer managed to transmit valuable information back to Germany; post-war, he became an admiral in the Federal German Navy's submarine service.

❏ On June 4, 1944, a U.S. Navy escort carrier group under Admiral D.V. Gallery (1901-77) captured *U-505*. Depthcharged to the surface and boarded, this submarine was the first foreign warship taken on the high seas by the U.S.N. since the War of 1812.

Travelling at the speed of its slowest ship, a convoy could often be outpaced by U-boats, which attacked by night.

A radar equipped PB4Y-1, the U.S. Navy's version of the Consolidated B-24 Liberator bomber, scans the Atlantic for U-boats.

'Wavy' livery makes the long range patrol plane harder to spot against an ocean background.

Desert victory: El Alamein

In June 1942 Rommel's *Panzerarmee Afrika* advanced into Egypt. British General Auchinleck's forces fell back to El Alamein, establishing a defence line between the coast and the Qattara Depression, an impenetrable marsh 64km (40mi) inland. Although outnumbered (90 tanks; but of better quality than Auchinleck's 160) Rommel attacked on July 1. Four weeks' fighting ended in stalemate; and a surprise attack by Rommel on August 30 was repulsed at Alam Halfa. General Alexander had now replaced Auchinleck, and British 8th Army was commanded by General Montgomery. While Rommel begged in vain for equipment that went instead to the Russian campaign, Montgomery built up his strength. A meticulous planner, he would not attack until he had total superiority. By October he had c.1,030 tanks (including 285 U.S. made Shermans) and 200,000 men, against c.600 German and Italian tanks (only 38 PzKw.IV, matching the Shermans) and 105,000 men, and was stronger in anti-tank weapons and air support. He attacked to the north of the line – clever displays of 'phantom' vehicles had suggested he would go south – on October 23. After a 600-gun barrage, armour and infantry advanced – but were halted by minefields and lost heavily. Rommel counterattacked savagely, but Montgomery calmly rethought his plans, regrouped his forces, and launched a knockout blow at Rommel's weakest point, his Italian allies, on November 2. With only 35 tanks left, hardly any petrol, and c.59,000 casualties, Rommel disengaged. In January 1943 he was driven back to Tunisia, ending the Axis threat to Egypt.

General Bernard Montgomery (here seen in 'bush hat' with Australian badge) took command of British 8th Army in August 1942. Post-war he was ennobled as Viscount Montgomery of Alamein.

Artillery duels were fought as the opponents manoeuvred. Here, an Axis shell falls short of a British battery.

Allied artillery fired over 1,000,000 shells at El Alamein, where the attack began with a huge barrage from guns like this British 25-pounder.

Field Marshal Rommel was much outnumbered in armour, guns, men and air support. But the 'Desert Fox' saved many of his men by a most skilful withdrawal.

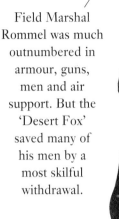

American-built tanks helped win the battle of El Alamein. Soon U.S. Army tanks (seen here with British infantry) were in Tunisia.

FACT FILE

❏ The U.S. M4 Sherman tank proved its worth in North Africa and was the workhorse of Allied armoured forces through World War II. Earlier models weighed 30 tonnes, with armour up to 102mm (4in) thick, mounted a 75mm (3in) gun, and had a maximum speed of 42kmh (26mph). Some 50,000 were built. The most numerous German tank, the PzKw.IV, also mounted a 75mm (3in) gun. It weighed 20 tonnes, with armour up to 90mm (3.5in) thick, and a top speed of 40kmh (25mph). Some 8,500 were built.

❏ The largest (but not the heaviest) aircraft of the war, the Messerschmitt Me 323 *Gigant* ('Giant'), was used to supply Axis troops in North Africa. Based on a transport glider design, with a load capacity of some 20 tonnes, it had six engines and a wingspan of 55m (181ft). Although it mounted up to seven machine guns and two cannon, it was a slow (217kmh/135mph), clumsy, death trap.

❏ Rommel's men and British 8th Army shared a favourite song, 'Lili Marlene', popularized before the war by the Swedish singer Lale Andersen. In the German Army's version, 'Lili' was a hooker plying her trade 'under the lantern, by the barrack gate'. In the British version, sung by Anne Shelton, she became a young girl waiting for her soldier boyfriend.

'Operation Torch'

Landing craft from an offshore armada ferry men and equipment of General Fredendall's U.S. 1st Division to the beaches at Oran, Algeria; November 8, 1942.

'Second Front Now!' demanded the hard-pressed U.S.S.R. from 1942, urging its Western allies to draw German strength from the East by invading mainland Europe. The Allies' first step was the conquest of French North Africa. In 'Operation Torch', November 7-8, 1942, task forces under overall command of General Eisenhower landed at Casablanca, on the Atlantic coast of Morocco, and in the Mediterranean at Oran and Algiers. Vichy French resistance was fierce but brief: the Vichy leader, Admiral Darlan, ordered a ceasefire on November 10, and soon many Vichy troops became 'Fighting French'. ('Free French' forces with the Allies were called 'Fighting French' from June 1942.) The Allies raced eastward into Tunisia, but hope of quick conquest faded as General von Arnim's 5th Panzer Army was reinforced from France and Sicily – and by Rommel's *Panzerarmee Afrika* (pursued by Mongomery's 8th Army) from Libya. On February 19, 1943, Rommel mauled the inexperienced U.S. 2nd Corps at Kasserine Pass. The Americans lost c.150 tanks and more than 6,000 men killed, wounded or captured. But Rommel's request for more Tiger I tanks, to strike deep into the Allied lines, was refused, and on March 6 he was defeated by Montgomery at Médenine. In March-April, U.S., British and French forces drove German-Italian defenders from the 'Mareth Line' and pinned them down on the Cape Bon peninsula. On May 11, having taken some 60,000 casualties (Allied casualties were c.75,000), 240,000 Axis troops surrendered. Allied control of North Africa opened the way for the invasion of Sicily and Italy.

This German tank will fight no more: but at Kasserine Pass, February 19, 1943, PzKw.IV and heavy Pzkw.VI Tiger tanks of *Panzerarmee Afrika*'s Assault Group destroyed a larger U.S. armoured force.

Troops landed at Oran faced determined Vichy French resistance; at Casablanca and Algiers, opposition was lighter.

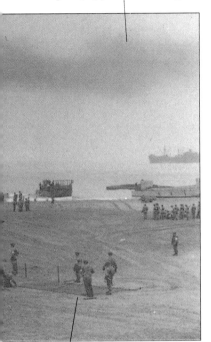

U.S. Army combat engineers lay down steel matting to stabilize the beach.

These 'Fighting French' soldiers travelled far to take part in 8th Army's attack on the Mareth Line. Under General Jacques Leclerc, they marched 2,400km (1,500mi) across the Sahara from French Equatorial Africa.

A recovery vehicle brings up the rear of an Allied supply convoy moving past the knocked out Tiger tank.

The map shows important sites in the Allied conquest of North Africa. Anglo-U.S. forces landed at Casablanca, Oran and Algiers; while 8th Army advanced from Tunisia. Axis survivors fled from Cape Bon to Sicily.

Map:
SICILY
MEDITERRANEAN SEA
Cape Bon
Algiers
Kasserine
Oran
TUNISIA
Mareth Line
Casablanca
ALGERIA
MOROCCO
LIBYA

❏ In 1942 about two-thirds of France was under German occupation. The remainder, called Vichy France from its capital, was governed by Marshal Henri Pétain (1856-1951) and others sympathetic to the Germans. Following 'Operation Torch', when many Frenchmen in North Africa joined the Allies, the Germans occupied all France.

❏ Just before 'Torch', U.S. General Mark Clark, Eisenhower's deputy, secretly landed from a British submarine near Algiers to persuade anti-Axis French officers to support the Allies. (He almost drowned when his small boat capsized, and said that one of its crew had yelled: 'Never mind the **** general; grab the **** oars!') Some claim that the Allies 'arranged' the assassination, on December 24, 1942, of Vichy commander Admiral Jean Darlan, trusted by neither side; but it is now generally believed that the assassin was a French Royalist fanatic.

❏ The 54 tonne PzKw.VI Tiger I tank, with an 88mm gun patterned on the famous 'eighty-eight' anti-aircraft gun, outclassed U.S. Lee and Sherman tanks at Kasserine. But Rommel had few of these formidable battlewagons (only c.1,300 were built in 1942-44), many of which went to elite *Waffen* S.S. formations. By late 1944, the lighter but more agile (and numerous) Allied tanks had drawn the Tiger's teeth.

Red fortresses: Stalingrad and Leningrad

Huge German howitzers or mortars, like this captured example, were used in the sieges of Stalingrad and other Soviet cities.

In June 1942, as German armies advanced on the oil-rich Caucasus region of the U.S.S.R., Hitler ordered the capture of Stalingrad on the Volga River. By August the city was encircled by General von Paulus's 6th Army. Hitler, obsessed with capturing 'Stalin's city', ordered all-out assault. Soviet General Chuikov's 62nd Army fought a stubborn house-to-house battle – aided, ironically, by massive German bombardments that smashed the city to rubble, creating good defensive positions. This gave Marshal Zhukov time to counterattack: in late November Russian armies encircled Stalingrad. Paulus might have broken out, but Hitler, told that the Luftwaffe could airlift in 500 tonnes of supplies daily (it averaged less than 80 tonnes), ordered him to hold on. German relief attempts were driven off, and on January 8, 1943, Rokossovsky attacked. Paulus, his men sick and starving, surrendered on January 31. About 140,000 Germans died at Stalingrad and c.91,000 were captured, along with c.1,500 tanks and 6,000 guns. Stalingrad turned the tide against Germany in the eastern sector; turning point in the northwest was the siege of Leningrad, encircled by German and Finnish armies in September 1941. Only an 'ice road' across frozen Lake Ladoga, crossed by trucks under artillery and air attack, saved the defenders of the U.S.S.R.'s second largest city from starvation in winter 1941-42. Even so, in the 880 day siege c.630,000 civilians starved to death, while c.200,000 were killed by enemy action. Some 200,000 Germans and Finns died in a series of savage battles to prevent the relief of the city, which was not accomplished until January 1944.

The body of a starvation victim is dragged to burial on an improvised sledge. Such sights were commonplace in besieged Leningrad, where the maximum food allowance, for soldiers and key workers, fell as low as 340g (12oz) per day.

Soviet soldiers at Stalingrad carry cheap, easily produced, *PPsh* sub-machine guns; these were ideal weapons for close-range fighting.

When the Germans took Leningrad's last railhead in November 1941, the Russians built an 'ice road' across frozen Lake Ladoga: the city's lifeline in winter 1941-42.

A Red Army man directs trucks on the 'ice road'. In 1941-42 some 53,000 tonnes of supplies came along it, often under heavy fire.

Bombardment reduced Stalingrad to ruins – in which the city's garrison held out stubbornly until a Soviet counterattack could be launched to raise the siege.

On the map (serving also as a locator for the campaigns described on *pages 38-39* and *60-61*) the red line shows the extent of German penetration into the U.S.S.R. at the time of the battle of Stalingrad, late 1942.

❑ Of c.91,000 Germans taken prisoner at Stalingrad, it is estimated that only about 6,000 survived captivity.

❑ One day before Paulus's surrender, Hitler promoted him Field Marshal, hoping it would inspire him to die 'heroically', by suicide, for propaganda purposes. In captivity, Paulus turned against the Führer and made anti-Nazi radio broadcasts. He gave evidence against German leaders at Nuremberg in 1945.

❑ Red Army Lieutenant General Andrei Vlasov (1900-46), captured during the Leningrad campaign, changed sides. He recruited other Russian prisoners into an anti-Soviet 'Army of Liberation', which saw combat in 1944-45. In May 1945 he changed sides once more, leading his renegade troops into Prague and taking it from the Germans. He then tried to surrender the city, and his force, to U.S. 7th Army. The Americans, in accordance with recent Allied political agreements, refused. Vlasov was handed over to the Soviets, who executed him.

❑ Although the heroic resistance at Stalingrad and Leningrad is still honoured in the U.S.S.R., the cities' names are not. 'De-Stalinization' after Stalin's death in 1953 saw Stalingrad renamed Volgograd. In 1991, when the U.S.S.R. itself fell apart, Leningrad decided to return to its pre-1914 name, St. Petersburg.

Kursk: greatest tank battle

A 'tank hunter', a heavy anti-tank gun on a tracked chassis, moves into action.

Typical of the self-propelled guns used by both sides at Kursk was the German *Nashorn* ('Rhino').

In 1943 Hitler called for a 'decisive victory' on the central Russian front. Field Marshal von Manstein's capture of Kharkov had created a 'bulge', the Kursk salient, in the Soviet lines. 'Operation Citadel' was to encircle and destroy two Soviet army groups in the salient. General Model's 9th Army, north of the salient, and General Hoth's 4th Panzer Army, to the south, had c.900,000 men, 2,700 tanks and 10,000 artillery pieces, supported by c.1,850 aircraft. But the slow German build-up allowed Marshal Zhukov, warned by the Swiss-based 'Lucy' spy ring, to assemble an even greater force. Around Kursk, protected by eight rings of minefields and anti-tank guns, Generals Rokossovsky and Vatutin (with General Konev's army in reserve) had c.1,300,000 men, 3,600 tanks, 20,000 guns and 2,400 planes. The Germans advanced on July 5, after a huge artillery bombardment, but only the outer Soviet lines were penetrated. Soviet anti-tank gunners found that the heavily armoured PzKw.V 'Panther' and PzKw.VI 'Tiger' tanks were vulnerable to attack from the rear; tank-busting '*Stormovik*' aircraft took heavy toll, while Yak-9 fighter planes mastered the Luftwaffe. On July 12, when the Germans made their final effort, some 1,300 tanks clashed in what was (until the Arab-Israeli War of 1973) the greatest armoured battle ever known. On July 13 Zhukov threw in his reserves, driving back the Germans with the loss of more than half their armour and aircraft and c.100,000 men. Soviet losses were equally high – but Hitler's last great offensive on the Eastern Front had been defeated.

The Red Army, able to sustain heavy losses, sometimes sent infantry ahead of tanks to locate minefields.

Soviet infantry advance alongside armour. The Red Army committed well over 1,000,000 men and some 3,600 tanks to the battle of Kursk.

Soviet 'tank riders' in training. All armed with sub-machine guns, they specialized in knocking out the enemy's anti-tank positions.

If this T-34 encounters an anti-tank gun, the 'tank riders' will dismount and charge it.

The T-34/85 medium tank entered service in 1940 and became the mainstay of Soviet armoured formations.

❏ The German advance was spearheaded by groups of heavy 'Tiger' tanks and 'Elefant' assault guns. The 67 tonne 'Elefant' Panzerjäger ('tank hunter') had armour up to 203mm (8in) thick and mounted an 88mm gun – but it was slow and clumsy, and in short range actions, as were many at Kursk, was quickly surrounded and knocked out by weight of numbers.

❏ Fast (50kmh/31mph), agile, and mounting a 76mm (later 85mm) gun, the 32 tonne Soviet T-34 is said by many experts to have been the best tank of World War II. More than 40,000 T-34s were built.

❏ 'Tank busting' aircraft played a major part on both sides at Kursk. The Soviet Ilyushin Il-2 'Stormovik' (below) was itself a 'flying tank': heavily armoured, mounting two 20mm cannon and carrying eight rockets or 365kg (800lb) of bombs in underwing racks. At Kursk a group of 'Stormoviks' flying the 'Circle of Death' (circling the target and attacking one by one, to prolong the assault) was credited with destroying 70 tanks in 20 minutes.

Into Italy: Sicily and Salerno

The map serves as a locator for the major events of the conquest of Italy (see also *pages 64-65*), from the invasion of Sicily, July 1943, to the German surrender on the Po River, May 1945.

Marshal Pietro Badoglio (1871-1956), who had since 1940 been opposed to Mussolini's handling of the war, took over the Italian government when the dictator fell in July 1943. He made peace with the Allies.

At the Casablanca Conference, January 1943, Churchill and Roosevelt decided the Allies' first step back into Europe would be the invasion of Sicily: 'Operation Husky'. On July 10, General Patton's U.S. 7th Army landed on Sicily's south coast, and Montgomery's British 8th Army on the southeast. Defending the island, Italian General Guzzoni had c.230,000 men. Many of his Italians were weary of war, but his German divisions fiercely resisted the Allied advance on the 'Etna Line', holding it while preparations were made for an Axis evacuation to Italy. By the time the Allies took Messina, August 17, some 100,000 German troops had been successfully evacuated.

But the Italians had had enough: Mussolini had been overthrown on July 25, and on September 3 his successor, Marshal Badoglio, made peace. This allowed the Allies to land unopposed on the eastern Italian mainland at Reggio and Taranto, and to launch 'Operation Avalanche', a landing at Salerno, on the west coast, to take Naples. But the Germans swiftly rushed reinforcements to Italy, and the landing by General Mark Clark's 5th Army (one U.S. and one British corps) on September 9 met stiff opposition, taking some 15,000 casualties. 'Carpet bombing' by Allied planes, and shelling by cruisers and battleships, helped Clark to hold his beachheads and break out towards Naples, which he took on October 1. Field Marshal Kesselring, German commander in Italy, fell back towards his defensive 'Gustav Line', south of Rome, determined to make the Allied conquest of Italy a long and bloody campaign.

Military supplies and the gear for handling them crowd the deck of a U.S. Navy attack transport – one unit in the Allied armada that lay off Sicily on the day of invasion; July 10, 1943.

The bow doors on a landing ship (note 20mm A.A.A.) open to unload men and materiel.

Life rafts were a vital part of the equipment of the slow, vulnerable landing ships.

❏ 'General Mafia's' part in the conquest of Sicily received little publicity. Acting, it is said, on the orders of U.S. Mafia boss Salvatore 'Lucky' Luciano, Don Calogero Vizzini (1877-1947), head of the Sicilian Mafia, ensured civilian support for the Allied invaders.

❏ Another mystery 'hero' was 'Major William Martin, Royal Marines'. Papers found with his body on a Spanish beach led German intelligence to expect an invasion of Sardinia rather than Sicily. The corpse of 'the man who never was' was that of an unknown civilian, with a briefcase containing fake 'top secret' documents, put into the Mediterranean from a British submarine.

❏ Late 1943 saw the first use of 'smart bombs' and 'guided missiles' by the Luftwaffe. The Ruhrstahl 1400 ('Fritz X'), a radio-controlled glider-bomb, sank the Italian battleship *Roma* on September 9, and damaged the cruiser USS *Savannah* and other Allied warships off Salerno. The Henschel Hs 293 was the first 'stand off' bomb: a small, pilotless aircraft launched from a 'mother plane' and radio guided to a target up to 24km (15mi) away. The 'Waterfall' ground-to-air guided missile carried a 300kg (660lb) warhead to c.15,240m (50,000ft). It could have been a deadly weapon, but its development was neglected in favour of the V-2 (*page 70*).

U.S. soldiers man the ramps as British troops come ashore at Salerno, first step on to the Italian mainland. Of c.85,000 Allied troops committed there, around 15,000 were killed or wounded.

A U.S. Navy LCS(S) – 'Landing Craft, Support (Small)' – comes alongside the transport. Note the rocket launching tubes mounted amidships. These 11m (36ft) craft were launched from landing ships to give close range fire in suppport of troops hitting the beaches.

Bloody 'sideshow': Italy, 1944-45

The plan to crush the Germans in Italy – an advance by General Clark's U.S. 5th Army and the British 8th Army up the west and east coasts respectively – seemed simple. But Kesselring made skilful use of Italy's rugged mountains and wide rivers in setting up defence lines. The Allies also had a fine commander, Field Marshal Alexander, but in overall strategy Italy was a 'sideshow', and his best troops and vital equipment were regularly taken to strengthen the invasion of western Europe. For months the Allies hammered at the 'Gustav Line' south of Rome. Bitter fighting centred on the Rapido River, where U.S. 36th Division was cut to pieces by German Panzer Grenadiers on January 20, and on the mountain of Monte Cassino, with its historic monastery. Four major battles were fought for Cassino, January-May 1944, the Allies taking c.115,000 casualties to the Germans' c.60,000. In an attempt to outflank the 'Gustav Line' and make a dash for Rome, 50,000 Allied troops landed at Anzio on January 22. But U.S. General Lucas was slow to advance from the beachhead: the Germans rushed up reinforcements and almost drove the Allies back into the sea. In May, Cassino fell and the Allies broke out from Anzio, securing Rome on June 5. Kesselring fell back to the 'Gothic Line', where there were more hard battles. In April 1945 the Germans were driven back across the Po River; on May 2 they surrendered. The Italian 'sideshow' cost the Allies c.312,000 casualties – but the Germans lost 536,000 men who might otherwise have turned the tide in western Europe.

British Field Marshal Sir Harold Alexander (later Earl Alexander of Tunis) (1891-1969) was overall commander of the Allied armies in Italy.

U.S. Army 'Ducks' (DUKWs; amphibious trucks) head towards transports off Anzio. 'Ducks' could carry 25-50 men or c.2,270kg (5,000lb) of cargo, at a top speed on land of about 80kmh (50mph).

The historic monastery on Monte Cassino lay in ruins after Allied bombing and savage ground fighting.

A Bofors 40mm A.A. gun is emplaced among the ruins at Cassino, site of four battles in January-May 1944.

The U.S. flag flies over Allied H.Q. in Rome, Italy's capital, taken on June 5, 1944.

Allied troops gather to celebrate in Rome – spared damage when the Germans declared it an undefended 'open city'.

❑ The Germans spared Rome much damage by declaring it an 'open city'. In contrast, Allied destruction of the historic monastery on Monte Cassino has been called a war crime. The Germans had not fortified the monastery – but when bombing reduced it to rubble they set up strong defences in its ruins. On May 18, 1944, these were taken by General Wladyslaw Anders's II Polish Corps. Men of the 12th Podolski Lancers raised the flag of Poland over the ruins.

❑ On October 13, 1943, Italy declared war on Germany – but some Italians still fought on the German side. Mussolini, rescued from imprisonment by German commandos, was declared head of the Fascist 'Salò Republic'. In April 1945, fleeing the Allied advance, Mussolini and his mistress Clara Petacci (1912-1945) were captured and shot by anti-Fascist partisans. Their bodies were put on display (below).

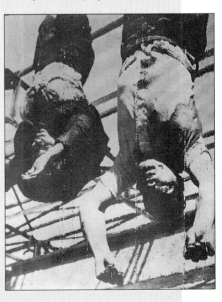

'Island hopping': the Pacific, 1943-44

After taking Guadalcanal, U.S. commanders adopted an overall strategy of westward 'island hopping' toward the Philippines. Islands needed as bases would be captured, others isolated to 'wither on the vine'. On November 20, 1943, 2nd Marine Division invaded Tarawa atoll, Gilbert Islands, 'stepping stone' to the Marshalls. Betio, the main island, was a fortress defended by c.5,000 troops. Many 'amtracs' (tracked landing vehicles) were lost on the reef round the lagoon, and heavily laden Marines made easy targets as they waded from reef to beach. But pre-invasion air and naval bombardment had so shaken the Japanese that they could not counterattack and destroy the beachhead. In 76 hours' close quarter combat the Marines took Betio at a cost of c.3,000 casualties; only 17 Japanese survived. Next objectives were Kwajalein and Eniwetok atolls in the western Marshalls, where U.S. bases would neutralize Japanese strongholds to the east. Carrier planes and naval gunfire softened up the defenders, and on February 1, 1944, 4th Marine Division hit Roi-Namur on the north of Kwajalein lagoon, while 7th Infantry Division landed to the south. Both were supported by artillery fire from islets seized the day before. Kwajalein's 87 islands were secured by February 6, when 41,000 U.S. troops (c.1,800 casualties) had landed. Almost all the 8,400 Japanese defenders died. Massive pre-invasion bombardment again minimized casualties on February 17, when Marines landed at Eniwetok. Of 3,500 defenders, only a few Korean conscripts survived; the Marines had c.1,200 casualties.

The wreck of a Japanese cargo ship lies rusting in a Pacific lagoon. Japan's merchant fleet had been almost totally destroyed by 1945.

More debris litters the beach. On many islands, Japanese garrisons isolated by the Allied advance almost starved.

A Lockheed P-38 Lightning fighter wears the livery seen in the European theatre. It distinguished itself in combat in the Pacific also.

The twin-boom layout of the very powerful P-38 won from the enemy the nickname of the 'Fork-tailed devil'.

Down the ramps of an LCI(L) ('Landing Craft Infantry (Large)'), U.S. soldiers storm on to a beachhead in the Southwest Pacific area.

❑ After Tarawa, the U.S.M.C.'s 8 tonne LVT 'Amtrac' (above) (AMphibious TRACtor) was given light armour plating. More than 18, 500 'Amtracs' – based on the 'Alligator' rescue craft of Florida's Everglades – were built during the war.

❑ 'Skip bombing' – attacking ships from low level, so bombs with delayed action fuses 'bounced' over the water to the target – proved a success in the battle of the Bismarck Sea, March 2-3, 1943. A convoy carrying c.7,000 Japanese to New Guinea was intercepted by an armada of U.S.A.A.F. and Australian bombers. Losing only five planes, the Allies sank six transports and four destroyers.

❑ Early in 1943 Admiral Yamamoto, Japan's naval supremo, visited the Solomons. 'Magic' code breaking revealed his itinerary, and on April 18 his aircraft was shot down by P-38 Lightning fighters from Guadalcanal. The ambush has been criticized (as was a British commando forces' attempt to kill Rommel in 1941) for breaking an 'unwritten rule' forbidding assassination of leaders and top commanders.

By day and by night

The British and U.S. air forces tried to cripple Germany by 'strategic bombing' – attacks on industrial centres to destroy factories and the morale of workers. In 1939-41 the R.A.F. had few heavy bombers and lacked the technical means for such 'precision' raids. By 1942, the R.A.F. had heavy Stirling and Lancaster bombers, the U.S. 8th Air Force's 'heavies' were based in Britain, and navigational aids and bomb sights had improved. The R.A.F. had lost heavily in daylight raids on industrial targets, so Air Marshal 'Bomber' Harris favoured 'area bombing': night attacks on big cities. On July 24-August 2, 1943, half of Hamburg was destroyed thus, killing c.40,000 people. U.S. General 'Hap' Arnold preferred daylight 'precision' attacks by high flying, well armed B-17s and B-24s. At first it seemed the British were right. Germany's 'Kammhuber Line' – a network of radar assisted A.A.A. and day and night fighters – destroyed many bombers. After 65 out of 291 U.S. bombers were lost in a raid on factories at Schweinfurt, October 14, 1943, 'precision' day bombing was limited, until the introduction of the P-51 Mustang in 1944 provided Allied bombers with permanent fighter escort. Then the Luftwaffe's fighter force was worn down, and bombing significantly damaged German war production. The cost was very high: in the British-U.S. 'Combined Bomber Offensive' of 1940-45, c.21,900 planes were lost and c.159,000 air crew killed. About 2,700,000 tonnes of bombs fell, devastating huge areas of German towns and killing c.700,000 civilians.

A 12.7mm (.50in) machine gun arms the ventral turret of a U.S. B-17 bomber.

The 'belly gunner' – often chosen for his small stature – had the most cramped and dangerous position in the aircraft.

The radio operator (left) and flight engineer (right) of a British bomber crew are seen after a mission in 1943.

The inflatable 'Mae West' lifejacket was named after a buxom American actress.

A P-51D Mustang (note 'teardrop' cockpit canopy) heads a homing flight after escort duty over Germany; 1944.

P-51 Mustangs entered service as long range, high level escorts for Allied bombers early in 1944.

The Avro Lancaster entered combat in March 1942 and became the mainstay of the R.A.F.'s night bombing offensive on Germany.

R.A.F. ground crew men 'bomb up' a Lancaster, while at the plane itself other technicians carry out pre-flight checks.

A Lancaster could carry a load of c.6,350-8,165kg (14,000-18,000lb) of bombs over a combat range of some 3,200km (2,000mi).

❑ The first '1,000 Bomber' raid was made on May 30-31, 1942. The R.A.F. sent its total bomber strength (1,046 planes; 40 lost) against Cologne, devastating 243ha (600 acres) of the city and causing about 5,500 casualties.

❑ The war's biggest bomb was the British 'Grand Slam,' a 9,980kg (22,000lb) 'deep penetration' weapon dropped by specially adapted Lancasters. It was first used in a raid on Bielefeld, Germany, March 14, 1945. This 'blockbuster' (a general nickname for very heavy bombs) produced a crater c.9m (30ft) deep and 38m (125ft) across.

❑ In Europe's most destructive air attack, some 1,200 British and U.S. bombers destroyed c.70 per cent of the historic city of Dresden on February 13-15, 1945. British night bombers used a high proportion of incendiaries, creating 'fire storms'. Dresden was crowded with refugees fleeing the Soviet advance: estimates of civilian dead range from 65,000 to more than 130,000.

❑ The casualty rates of R.A.F. Bomber Command and U.S. 8th Air Force were among the highest of the war. It was estimated that three out of every four Bomber Command air crew members would be killed, wounded or captured. Hitler considered having all captured bomber crews shot.

'V' is for vengeance

The Fieseler Fi 103 (V-1) 'flying bomb' was sometimes air launched from beneath a Heinkel He 111 bomber.

The German A-4 rocket (usually called the V-2) had a c.975kg (2,145lb) Amatol warhead that detonated on impact.

On June 13, 1944, Londoners heard a sound in the sky 'like a motorcycle running underwater'. The noise stopped – and six people died, first victims of *Vergeltungswaffen Eins* ('Vengeance Weapon One'; V-1), nicknamed the 'Doodlebug'. This stub-winged, pilotless aircraft, with a pulse jet engine giving a top speed of c.644kmh (400mph), carried a one-tonne warhead to a range of 402km (250mi). Launched from a ski-ramp (occasionally from a 'mother' aircraft), it had a guidance system that put it into a dive over the target, most often London or the Allied supply port of Antwerp. It proved vulnerable to fighter interception and proximity fused A.A.A., but of c.9,000 aimed at London, c.2,400 hit, killing 6,184 people. Most V-1 launching sites were destroyed in the Allied advance from Normandy.

From September 1944 Germany deployed the V-2 (A-4), the world's first ballistic missile. This 13 tonne rocket, launched from a mobile trailer, carried a one-tonne warhead. Rising to a height of c.96km (60mi), it ended its flight (range c.320km/200mi) in a dive at 3,840kmh (2,386mph), so there was no defence against it. But it was inaccurate and subject to mechanical failure. Again, London (hit by 518 out of 1,115 V-1s that fell in Britain, killing 2,724 people) and Antwerp (1, 341 hits; c.30,000 casualties) were major targets. Germany would have done better to concentrate on its jet aircraft programme. The Messerschmitt Me 262 was the most formidable fighter of the war, but Hitler's order for its development as a tactical bomber delayed its combat debut until July 1944, about the same time as the R.A.F.'s Meteor jet.

The 14m (46ft) long supersonic guided missile had a liquid-fuelled engine. Post-war, it was studied by U.S. scientists for the fledgling space programme.

This A-4/V-2 stands ready to be launched from a *Meillerwagen*: an easily mobile platform that meant no permanent launch site was needed.

U.S. personnel inspect a damaged Messerschmitt Me 262 jet fighter. It entered combat too late significantly to affect the course of the war.

Seen beside the V-1 is one of the wire-wound air bottles that 'blew' fuel to its pulse jet power unit.

The Me 262's twin turbojets gave it a top speed of c.869kmh (540mph). It was armed with four 30mm cannon and 24 rockets.

Although capable of c.644kmh (400mph), in flight (inset) the 'doodlebug' proved vulnerable both to intercepting fighters and A.A.A.

❏ Hanna Reitsch (1912-79), the only woman to win the Iron Cross in World War II, flight tested both a piloted version of the V-1 flying bomb and the Me 163 rocket fighter.

❏ Germany hoped to use rockets against American cities. A plan to launch V-2s from special canisters towed within range of the U.S. mainland by U-boats came to nothing. The two-stage A9/A10 rocket, using a booster vehicle to give a winged V-2 a range of some 4,800km (3,000mi), never got beyond prototype.

❏ Germany's 'V-3', codenamed 'High Pressure Pump' or 'Millipede', was a 50-barrelled gun with a multi-chamber 'boost' system, capable of firing finned missiles to a range of c.280km (175mi). Late in 1944, just before its completion, the Allies captured its emplacement near Calais, France.

❏ The first jet-versus-jet combat took place on August 4, 1944, when an R.A.F. Gloster Meteor (prototype below) destroyed a V-1. The tactic (often used against the V-1) was to fly alongside and flip up a wingtip, to send the missile diving into the Channel.

The 'D-Day' landings

On 'D-Day', June 6, 1944, Allied armies stormed Hitler's 'Fortress Europe'. The invasion had been prepared from early 1943, when British General Sir Frederick Morgan was made head of Anglo-U.S. planning for 'Operation Overlord'. In December 1943 General Eisenhower was named Supreme Commander. The Allies had to muster forces for the greatest combined operation in history without alerting the Germans to the place of the invasion. 'Ghost armies', fake airfields and dummy armour parks in Britain suggested that the target was the Pas de Calais area, or even Scandinavia. At 0200 hours on June 6, parachute and glider troops dropped on the flanks and rear of the Normandy invasion area to disrupt defences and seize vital bridges. An armada of some 4,000 ships was already crossing the Channel. Landings began at 0630 hours, when U.S. 1st Army hit 'Omaha' and 'Utah' beaches. The 23,000 men landed at 'Utah' on the first day took only 200 casualties; at 'Bloody Omaha', overlooked by high cliffs, 37,000 attackers had c.4,500 casualties. Farther east, British troops, on 'Gold' and 'Sword' beaches, and Canadians, at 'Juno', had fairly light losses. Allied planes flew c.14,000 sorties; 600 warships patrolled the Channel. By nightfall some 155,000 men (c.10,500 casualties) had been put ashore and an advance inland towards Caen and Bayeux had begun. Hitler still believed 'D-Day' was a feint; that the 'real' invasion would be made in the Pas de Calais. Forces that might have pinned down the Allies near the beaches were held back to meet that threat.

U.S. General Eisenhower, Supreme Allied Commander, bravely decided to invade on June 6 in spite of the risk of bad weather in the English Channel.

British Air Chief Marshal Tedder (1890-1967) was 'Ike's' Deputy Supreme Commander from 1943 to the war's end.

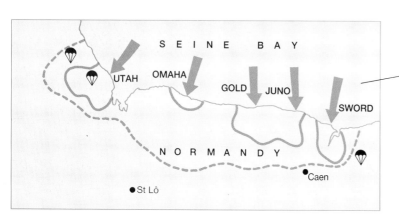

S E I N E   B A Y

UTAH   OMAHA

GOLD   JUNO

SWORD

N O R M A N D Y

Caen

St Lô

June 6, 1944. After airborne drops, U.S. 1st Army landed at 'Utah' and 'Omaha'; British and Canadian troops at 'Gold', 'Juno' and 'Sword'. Solid lines show areas won on 'D-Day'; broken line the desired perimeter.

A U.S. Martin B-26 Marauder bomber over the beaches on 'D-Day' is just one of more than 10,000 Allied aircraft deployed to cover the landings.

Landing craft are strewn along the beach on the morning of June 6, 1945. All looks calm in this aerial view – but the Allies took more than 10,000 casualties.

U.S. soldiers train off the British coast for the 'D-Day' landings. In April 1944 some 600 G.I.s died when German torpedo boats sank landing craft like that seen here, off Slapton Sands, Devon.

More than 4,000 craft like this British LCA (Landing Craft, Assault) were used on 'D-Day.'

❏ 'Hobo's Funnies' saved many casualties on D-Day. These were the tanks of British General Percy Hobart's 79th Armoured Division, specially adapted for amphibious landings, mine clearance, flamethrowing, demolition of obstacles, track and bridge laying and other tasks. General Gerow, U.S. commander at 'Bloody Omaha' beach, had refused to receive help from the 'funnies'.

❏ By September 15, 1944, more than 2,000,000 Allied servicemen had landed in France. Some 40,000 were killed, and 190,000 wounded or missing. German casualties are put as high as 700,000.

❏ Unsung heroes of the breakout from Normandy were the loaders and drivers, many black (below), of the U.S. 'Red Ball Express'. Driving flat out on a one-way 'loop', until either they or their trucks collapsed from exhaustion, they rushed vital supplies to the front from the depot at Saint-Lô. In August-October 1944, their 6,000 trucks hauled 400,000 tonnes of supplies.

Resistance in Europe

In 1941 Hitler's empire extended from the Channel coast into the U.S.S.R. and from Scandinavia to North Africa. Many men and women fled Nazi-occupied countries to join the Allies. 'Fighting French' rallied around General de Gaulle; Poles, Czechs, Norwegians and others formed independent Allied combat units. Those who remained had a choice between collaboration – *Ausland* ('Foreign') units of the *Waffen*-S.S. gained recruits in France, Holland, Belgium and Eastern Europe – apathy or resistance. Passive resistance, refusal to aid the occupiers, worked best in Denmark, where ruler and government had not fled abroad but remained as a symbol of independence. Active resistance reached its height in Eastern Europe, where Nazi racial persecution was cruellest. In Yugoslavia large 'partisan' armies tied down many German troops. The Yugoslav Communist leader (Josip Broz) Tito, with 800,000 troops by 1945, at the same time fought a civil war against the anti-Nazi 'Chetniks', Yugoslav Royalists. French resistance, too, was hampered by an internal struggle between Communists and anti-Communists. Nevertheless, it carried out successful sabotage campaigns and, after D-Day, openly rose in arms.

Inside Germany, opposition to Hitler centred on military men disillusioned with his war leadership. Several senior commanders committed suicide or were executed after the failure of the 'July Plot' of 1944, when a bomb planted by Colonel Count von Stauffenberg narrowly failed to kill Hitler at his headquarters in East Prussia.

A tricolour badge marks a French collaborator who has volunteered to serve in the German Army.

The Resistance fighters of Paris, Communists and Gaullists alike, rose openly against the occupying force on August 19, 1944.

These Frenchmen in German uniforms have enrolled for the Nazis' 'Crusade against Bolshevism'.

General Charles de Gaulle (1890-1970) led a French armoured division against the German invasion in 1940. After France's collapse, he played a major part in rallying the 'Free French' who fought on alongside the Allies.

After liberation, a shaven head is the punishment for this French woman, who carries a baby fathered by a German soldier.

In late 1944, a hostile crowd jeers French women accused of giving aid and comfort to the German occupation forces.

An American-built tank shelters armed Parisians as they trade shots with Germans barricaded in a building.

The great 'turkey shoot'

Throughout the war, Japanese naval strategy aimed at a 'decisive battle'. In June 1944, when U.S. Admiral Nimitz committed much of his fleet to support the invasion of the Marianas (Saipan, Tinian, Guam), Admiral Ozawa sought this showdown. He deployed nine aircraft carriers (c.450 planes) against Admiral Mitscher's Task Force 58 (15 carriers; c.890 planes), and expected help from aircraft based on Guam – but most had been destroyed by U.S. carrier strikes. Early on June 19, Ozawa launched c.370 planes. Directed by radar, in which the U.S.N. far excelled the I.J.N., Mitscher's aircraft intercepted and, in what U.S. flyers named the 'Great Marianas Turkey Shoot', shot down c.240 for the loss of only 29 U.S. aircraft. U.S. submarines sank two of Ozawa's carriers. Mitscher gambled on a night attack on the retreating Japanese, launching 216 planes at very long range. Only 20 U.S. aircraft were shot down as they sank one carrier, damaged another, and destroyed 65 more Japanese planes. Although c.70 U.S. aircraft 'ditched' or crashed on their carriers when returning in darkness, many of their crews survived. Japan's loss of veteran flyers was even more serious than that of aircraft: the I.J.N.'s carriers were a spent force and the Philippine Sea was the last of the great carrier-against-carrier battles. With her merchant fleet almost completely destroyed by U.S. submarines – which sank 1,153 merchantmen, totaling c.4,900,000 tonnes, in 1941-45 – and her harbours blocked by aerial minelaying, Japan was denied the fuel and materials needed for large offensive operations.

A U.S. Navy pilot 'wing walks' to safety after landing his damaged plane aboard a carrier.

A firefighting team moves in to try to salvage the burning Grumman F6F Hellcat fighter.

While carrier fighters destroyed Japan's naval air power, U.S. bombers like this B-25 Mitchell hammered shipping and shore installations.

Spray breaks over the forward casing and the 127mm (5in) gun of a U.S. Navy 'T' (*Tambor*) Class submarine. American submarines destroyed most of Japan's merchant fleet.

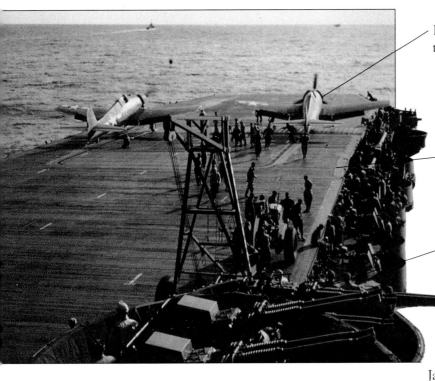

F6F Hellcat fighters, like these awaiting take off on U.S.S. *Enterprise*, were the victors in the 'Great Marianas Turkey Shoot'.

Enterprise, a heavy carrier, could carry and operate about 100 aircraft.

These 40mm guns were part of a carrier's defence against aircraft.

Harbour works and air strips at Rabaul, Japan's key base in the New Guinea-Solomons area, blaze after a raid by bombers of U.S. 5th Air Force.

A Japanese freighter is hard hit by the B-25's mast level strike.

FACT FILE

❏ Although it was one of the finest fighters of all time, Japan's Mitsubishi A6M 'Zero' (more than 10,000 built) was by 1944 outclassed by U.S. fighters like the Grumman F6F Hellcat and Vought F4U Corsair. But its agility was such that, until the war's end, U.S. pilots' combat instructions carried the emphatic warning: 'NEVER DOGFIGHT WITH A ZERO!'

❏ U.S. 'ace' submariner of the Pacific War was Commander (later Rear Admiral) Richard H. O'Kane (b.1911). His USS *Tang* sank 24 Japanese ships (totaling 93,824 tonnes) in five patrols – and then sank herself! On October 25,1944, one of *Tang*'s own torpedoes doubled back on its run and struck her. O'Kane was one of only eight survivors from the unlucky boat.

❏ Heavy cruiser USS *Indianapolis* (Captain Charles B. McVay) was sunk on July 29, 1945, by Japanese submarine *I-58* (Commander Hashimoto). Some 350 men went down with her; others took to the sea where, because of garbled communications, c.530 died from exposure and shark attack in three days before rescue arrived. Post-war, Hashimoto gave evidence at McVay's court martial for hazarding his ship by not taking proper anti-submarine precautions. McVay was found guilty, but his sentence was not put into effect.

'Forgotten armies': Burma, 1941-45

Earlier in the war neither side regarded Burma as a major theatre: dispirited British troops there called themselves the 'Forgotten Army'. The Japanese had invaded Burma in December 1941 – forcing Anglo-Indian and Chinese armies (the latter under U.S. General Joseph Stilwell) to retreat swiftly to India – mainly to capture the port of Rangoon and close the 'Burma Road', Allied supply route to China. From late 1942, however, they planned to invade India, hoping its people would rise against British rule. A British offensive on the Arakan coast early in 1943 failed, but raids by General Orde Wingate's 'Chindit' commandos, penetrating deep into enemy lines, raised morale by proving the Japanese were not 'supermen' in jungle fighting. The Japanese offensive early in 1944 was opposed by larger forces (General 'Bill' Slim's British 14th Army and Stilwell's Chinese Army had c.650,000 men against c.320,000 Japanese), whose control of the air allowed speedy supply and reinforcement. At Kohima-Imphal, a sprawling battle on the Indo-Burmese border in March-June 1944, Slim decisively defeated General Mutaguchi's 15th Army (53,000 casualties). Farther east, Stilwell's Chinese, aided by the Chindit-style operations of U.S. General Frank D. Merrill's 5307th Composite Unit ('Merrill's Marauders'), captured Myitkyina and reopened the supply route to China. The Allies advanced overland towards Mandalay (taken in March 1945), while a new Arakan offensive culminated in an amphibious move on Rangoon (secured May 1945). The Japanese lost heavily as they retreated towards Malaya across the Sittang River.

British Major General Orde Wingate (1903-44); leader of jungle commandos.

Wingate's 'Chindits' – seen here in jungle 'uniform' – made long marches, sometimes aided by air drops, to strike behind Japanese lines.

Chinese soldiers driven from Burma by the Japanese attack in 1942 returned as tough jungle fighters after training under U.S. General Stilwell in India.

At Ramgarh, India, Stilwell's Chinese troops learned to handle U.S. equipment like this 75mm M1 pack howitzer.

The Allied 'forgotten armies' in Burma fought the Japanese in dense tropical growth like this.

General Joseph Stilwell (1883-1946), Allied second in command in China-Burma-India in 1943-44, was an effective but cantankerous leader. His sharp tongue gained him the nickname of 'Vinegar Joe'.

In 1942, the 60-year-old Stilwell personally led his Chinese soldiers' 225km (140mi) 'walk out' from Burma.

❏ The last charge in the long and glorious history of British horsed cavalry is said to have been made in Burma on March 18, 1942. With sabre drawn, Captain Arthur Sandeman, Central India Horse, led 100 troopers of the Burmese Frontier Force against Japanese machine gun nests near the Sittang River. Sandeman was killed and his men driven back.

❏ Kohima-Imphal saw one of the war's greatest 'air lifts', as the Allies flew in 6,000 tonnes of supplies (including 43 million cigarettes). But although the campaign spread over a wide area, a vital action at Kohima itself was fought across a tennis court. Defending an all-weather highway across the mountainous Indo-Burmese frontier, c.500 men (c.300 casualties) of the Royal West Kent Regiment held the court, in the grounds of the District Commissioner's residence, against c.6,000 Japanese for 15 days until relieved.

❏ Anglo-Indian troops landed on Ramree Island, off Akyab, on January 21, 1945. On February 19, c.1,000 Japanese made a last stand in a mangrove swamp. Attracted by blood from the wounded, an army of estuarine crocodiles swarmed in from the Bay of Bengal. Many Japanese were dragged away, or committed suicide to escape the fearsome predators. Next day the Allies found only 30 survivors.

Arnhem: one drop too many

General Eisenhower decided the Allied advance to the Rhine should be on a 'broad front'. He was opposed by Montgomery and U.S. General Patton, who favoured 'knifelike thrusts' against the retreating Germans. Eisenhower's strategy prevailed, but he agreed to let Montgomery use U.S. General Lewis Brereton's 1st Allied Airborne Army (parachute and glider troops) to lay an 'airborne carpet' through Holland. In 'Operation Market Garden', three simultaneous airborne attacks were to secure bridges over canals near Eindhoven; on the Maas and Waal Rivers at Grave and Nijmegen; and on the Lower Rhine at Arnhem; creating a 72km (45mi) long corridor for a lightning advance by the armour of British XXX Corps. On September 17, 1944, U.S. 101st Airborne Division seized the Eindhoven bridges, and U.S. 82nd Airborne Division ('Screaming Eagles') dropped successfully at Grave and advanced on Nijmegen. But the British-Polish drops at Arnhem were poorly planned, and Montgomery had ignored intelligence warnings of strong German forces in the area. General Urquhart's 1st Airborne Division fought its way to the bridge only to be surrounded by S.S. panzer units. North of Nijmegen, where 82nd Airborne and the British Guards Armoured Division stormed the bridge on September 19, XXX Corps' advance was slow. In spite of air re-supply and reinforcement, in which many low-flying transport planes were downed by A.A.A., Urquhart's paratroopers were driven from the Arnhem bridge on September 21 and trapped north of the river. On September 25, c.2,400 survivors escaped across the river; some 7,800 were killed, wounded or captured.

A soldier of the British Army's Glider Pilot Regiment in training. More than 1,500 gliders, tugs (towing aircraft) and transport aircraft were needed for 'Operation Market Garden'.

The training glider is much smaller than those used in 'Market Garden'. There, the British Horsa could carry some 30 men; the U.S. Waco, 15 troops or c.1,680kg (3,700lb) of cargo.

Alert for enemy snipers, men of a U.S. airborne infantry unit advance along a ruined street in a Dutch town.

A supply canister is air dropped at Arnhem, where many low-flying Allied transport aircraft were downed by A.A.A.

Jeeps were sometimes landed in gliders, or sometimes dropped by parachute.

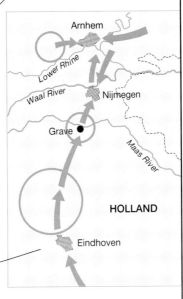

Fierce street battles raged along roads from Nijmegen, as U.S. airborne troops and British armoured units tried to fight their way to the men trapped at Arnhem.

'Market Garden' involved Allied airborne landings at Eindhoven, Grave, Nijmegen and Arnhem. German counterattacks came at Arnhem and Nijmegen.

FACT FILE

❏ Glider operations, which played an important part in 'Market Garden', were pioneered by the Germans. On May 10, 1940, 75 German combat engineers landed in gliders on the concrete covering of Fort Eben Emael, Belgium. Disabling its gun and observation turrets with hollow-charge explosives, they enabled the 'impregnable' fort to be taken within 30 hours.

❏ British paratroopers are still sometimes called 'Red Devils'. They got the nickname from German reports which spoke with admiration of 'those devils in red berets', outnumbered and lightly armed, who inflicted c.3,300 casualties on German armoured units at Arnhem.

❏ The British at Arnhem took on tanks with the PIAT (Projector Infantry Anti-Tank), a heavy (16kg/35 lb), clumsy weapon that threw a 1.1kg (2.5lb) bomb to an effective range (against tanks) of only 105m (115yd). Far better was the U.S. 'bazooka' rocket launcher, weighing only 5.9kg (13lb) and with twice the range. 'Bazookas' sent to the U.S.S.R. in 1942 were captured by the Germans, who modelled their tank-killing *Raketen Panzerbuchse* 54, firing a 3.2kg (7lb) rocket to 150m (165yd), on the U.S. weapon. The German *Panzerfaust* of 1945 was a cheaply made, one-shot, disposable projector with a range of only c.32m (35yd) – a near suicidal weapon.

Battle of 'the Bulge'

Late in 1944, as the Allies advanced across Belgium to the Rhine, Hitler planned a great offensive to drive a wedge into their 'broad front', split their armies and seize their chief supply port of Antwerp. He plundered Germany's reserves to mass three armies (c.250,000 men; 1,000 tanks and self propelled guns) under Field Marshal von Rundstedt. The main thrust was made (as in 1940) through the hilly, wooded Ardennes. Panzers crashed through the mist-shrouded, snowy forests to strike the thinly held line of U.S. 1st Army on December 16. Taken by surprise, the Allies fell back (although an attempt to spread panic behind their lines by infiltrating c.150 men of S.S. Colonel Otto Skorzeny's 'Special Forces', in U.S. uniforms, failed). On December 19, 8,000 men of U.S. 106th Division surrendered at the Schnee Eifel ridge. The panzers created a great 'bulge' encompassing the Allied communications centres of St Vith (which fell on December 27) and Bastogne, heroically defended by U.S. 10th Armored and 101st Airborne Divisions. Foul weather prevented the Allies from using the full weight of their air power. But lack of fuel slowed the German armour. General Patton's U.S. 3rd Army raced up from the south to relieve Bastogne on December 26; General 'Lightning Joe' Collins' U.S. VII Corps counterattacked in the north; and improved weather unleashed rocket firing planes – U.S. P-47 Thunderbolts and British Hawker Typhoons – against the panzers. By late January, when the Germans withdrew, the 'battle of the Bulge' had cost them c.90,000 men and 600 tanks; Allied losses were c.70,000 men and 733 tanks.

Von Rundstedt threw the best men he had left – like this battle hardened veteran – into the Ardennes.

In weatherproof overalls against the icy conditions in the 'Bulge', this German trooper carries an entrenching tool for digging in. Note the fighting knife tucked into his breast pack, and the belt of ammunition for a light machine gun.

A droppable fuel tank gave the Thunderbolt a range of some 3,220km (2,000mi), but as an escort fighter it was largely superseded by the P-51 Mustang.

Pilots who flew Thunderbolts, the largest and heaviest fighters of World War II, called them 'Jugs' (short for 'Juggernauts').

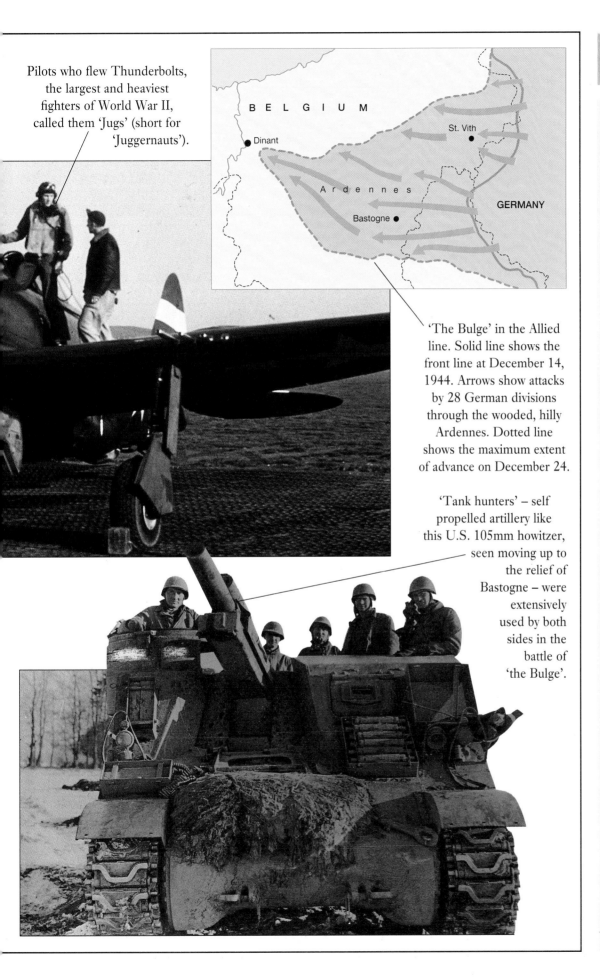

'The Bulge' in the Allied line. Solid line shows the front line at December 14, 1944. Arrows show attacks by 28 German divisions through the wooded, hilly Ardennes. Dotted line shows the maximum extent of advance on December 24.

'Tank hunters' – self propelled artillery like this U.S. 105mm howitzer, seen moving up to the relief of Bastogne – were extensively used by both sides in the battle of 'the Bulge'.

FACT FILE

❏ Surrounded by much larger German forces at Bastogne, U.S. General Anthony C. McAuliffe (1898-1975) (above) was formally called upon to surrender. His answer has passed into military legend: 'To the German commander: NUTS!'

❏ Penetration of the 'Bulge' was spearheaded by S.S. Lieutenant Colonel Joachim Peiper's panzers. At Malmédy, on December 17, Peiper's men murdered 86 U.S. prisoners. Post-war, Peiper was sentenced to death for the 'Malmédy massacre' and similar crimes, but reprieved on a legal technicality and freed in 1957. In 1976 he died mysteriously in a fire; perhaps the victim of vengeful French Resistance veterans.

❏ The self propelled gun was basically a heavy anti-tank gun or howitzer mounted on a tank chassis. Typical were the German *Nashorn* ('Rhinoceros'), with an 88mm (3.5in) anti-tank gun on a PzKw.IV chassis, and the massive *Jagdtiger* ('Hunting Tiger') tank destroyer, with a 128mm (5in) gun on a PzKw.VI Tiger II chassis.

Over the Rhine

Although weakened by the 'battle of the Bulge', German forces on the 'West Wall' (or 'Siegfried Line'), a 5km (3mi) deep belt of fortifications along Germany's western border, stoutly opposed the Allied advance. In February-March 1945 the Wall was breached and the Allies approached the Rhine River, last barrier to the heartland of Hitler's 'Thousand Year Reich'. It seemed certain the Germans would have destroyed all bridges over the great river, forcing the Allies into costly amphibious crossings under fire. But on March 7, a patrol of U.S. 1st Army reached the Ludendorff railway bridge at Remagen, near Cologne, just as German combat engineers prepared to blow it up. Demolition charges exploded as U.S. tanks and infantry charged across, but the bridge still stood: by the end of the day, c.8,000 U.S. troops had crossed to establish a foothold on the east bank. This allowed construction of two temporary bridges (under heavy air and artillery bombardment, including V-2 rockets and 'frogmen' who swam down the river with small mines), so that when the Ludendorff bridge collapsed 10 days later men and armour continued to pour across. Later in March, amphibious assault crossings secured more bridgeheads: the first, at Oppenheim to the south, on March 22-23 by Patton's U.S. 3rd Army. (Patton rejoiced at having beaten his British rival Montgomery, whose 1st Canadian Army crossed near Düsseldorf, to the north, on March 23-24.) By early April seven Allied armies were across the Rhine, at a cost of some 23,000 casualties. German losses (c.90,000 casualties; 259,000 prisoners) were such that the end of the war was in plain sight.

A smoke screen protects assault boats of U.S. 5th Army on the troubled waters of the Rhine; March, 1945.

U.S. General George S. 'Blood and Guts' Patton (1885-1945) commanded the fastest drive into Germany in 1945. His 3rd Army was codenamed 'Lucky'.

Pontoon bridges like this, under construction by U.S. Army engineers, continued to carry Allied forces across the Rhine at Remagen after the collapse of the Ludendorff Bridge.

❏ Hitler not only ordered the Rhine bridges destroyed (four officers were executed for the failure at Remagen) – on March 19 he demanded a 'scorched earth' policy for the destruction of everything of value in Germany (industry, communications, crops and buildings) in the case of Allied victory. More realistic German leaders, headed by Armaments Minister Albert Speer (1905-81), ensured that this command was not obeyed.

❏ Advancing from the Rhine, U.S. 1st and 9th Armies trapped Field Marshal Walther Model's Army Group B in the 'Ruhr Pocket'. On April 17, Model shot himself. His last order was that his men should decide for themselves whether to fight on, go home or surrender. The c.325,000 who surrendered (below) included 30 generals.

❏ U.S. General Patton had carried the ivory handled pistols that were his 'trade mark' since using them in close-quarter fighting during Pershing's Mexican Punitive Expedition of 1916-17.

The American flag flies over one of the towers of the Ludendorff Bridge at Remagen, seized by U.S. 9th Armored Division on March 7, 1945, as the Allies' first Rhine crossing.

Large, flat bottomed, barges ('pontoons'), buoyed up by inflatable chambers, support the metal framework and matting of the bridge. Combat engineers often worked under heavy fire.

Last days of the Reich

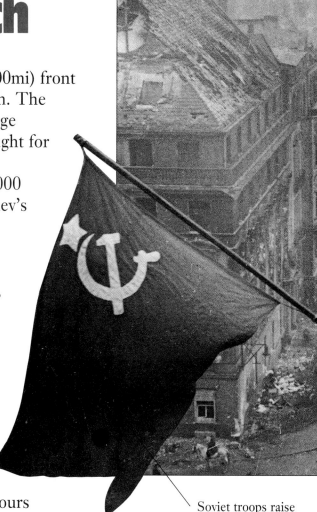

From late 1943 Soviet armies advanced along an 1,300km (800mi) front extending from Latvia in the north to Yugoslavia in the south. The U.S.S.R., with enormous reserves of manpower, could afford huge losses; but Hitler's order that every metre of ground must be fought for prevented his generals from preserving their forces by strategic withdrawal, and in June-November 1944 Germany lost c.1,000,000 men on the East Front. On April 25, 1945, men of General Konev's 1st Ukrainian Front met U.S. 1st Army at Torgau on the Elbe River. On the same day, farther north, Konev's armies and Zhukov's 1st Belorussian Front completed the encirclement of Berlin. Zhukov, in overall command, mustered c.2,500,000 men, 7,000 tanks, 52,000 guns and overwhelming air power. Defending Berlin and its 2,000,000 civilians were c.1,250,000 troops – and the *Volkssturm* ('People's Militia') of pensioners and Hitler Youth teenagers. From late April into May, a Soviet street by street advance reduced Berlin to rubble. On April 30, as Russian shells shook the massive walls of his '*Führerbunker*' under the Reich Chancellery, Hitler (with his mistress Eva Braun, whom he had married a few hours before) committed suicide. On May 2, General Helmuth Weidling surrendered his remaining men to the Soviets: German military casualties may have totalled more than 1,000,000; the Soviets admitted 304,000 casualties (the true figure was probably double); countless civilians died in the fighting and afterwards, as Zhukov's troops raped and looted. On May 7, at Reims, and May 8, in Berlin itself, General Jodl and Field Marshal Keitel signed the final acts of Germany's unconditional surrender.

Soviet troops raise a victory banner over the ruins of the *Reichstag* (German Parliament): a historic act at 1425 hours, April 30, 1945.

Fearing that he would be captured by the Red Army, Adolf Hitler shot himself on April 30, 1945.

Eva Braun (1912-45), Hitler's mistress for 12 years, became his wife on April 29, 1945. Next day she took poison and died at his side in Berlin.

Soviet armies fought their way street by street into Berlin. By the time the city surrendered on May 2, 1945, most of it lay in ruins.

General Alfred Jodl, German Chief of Staff (hanged for war crimes in 1946), signs the surrender agreement at Reims.

Other German cities suffered as severely as Berlin. Here, G.I.s and German civilians meet in a shattered street in Cologne.

FACT FILE

❑ Some historians condemn Eisenhower (above; with Air Marshal Tedder) for agreeing too readily that the Soviets, rather than the Allies, should take Berlin. The Allied commander wished to commit substantial forces farther south, where it was believed fanatical Nazis had prepared the 'National Redoubt', an Alpine fortress. They had not; nor did the activities of 'Werewolves', Nazi guerrilla fighters, much trouble Allied invasion and occupation troops.

❑ One thing cheered Hitler's last days: the death of President Roosevelt on April 12, 1945 – which Hitler hoped would signal a breach between the Western allies and the U.S.S.R. The seeds of the post-1945 'Cold War' between the Soviets and the West were sown at the Yalta Conference, February 11-14, 1945, where the ailing Roosevelt was persuaded by Stalin that the U.S.S.R. would bring 'democracy' to eastern Europe if it was allowed to have a free hand there.

Holocaust

Barbed wire, watch towers and armed guards: a scene typical of the Nazi concentration camps.

Germany's first 'concentration camp' for the imprisonment of 'enemies of the state' opened at Dachau on March 20, 1933, immediately after Hitler took power. He denounced the Jewish people as the prime source of Germany's troubles. German Jews were deprived of civil rights by the 'Nuremberg Laws' of 1935, and many fled abroad; those who remained were humiliated, plundered, and increasingly swelled the number of concentration camp inmates (along with 'undesirables', such as Gypsies, gay people and members of pacifist religious sects).

The conquest of Poland brought c.3,000,000 more Jews within the Reich; the attack on the U.S.S.R. many more. The Nazis agreed on a 'final solution of the Jewish problem': the extermination of European Jewry. The policy was directed by Heinrich Himmler (committed suicide in 1945) – a dull, flabby bureaucrat, whom to call 'evil' is to credit with too much humanity – with such helpers as Reinhard Heydrich (assassinated by Czech partisans in 1942); and Adolf Eichmann (hanged in Israel in 1962, after being snatched from hiding in Argentina). Out of a European Jewish population of c.8.3 million, more than 5 million died. Tens of thousands of other prisoners shared their agony: gassed, shot, tortured to death in obscene 'scientific research', starved or dying of disease in the vile conditions of the camps. At Nuremberg, in 1945-46, an International Military Tribunal tried 21 Nazi leaders for 'war crimes': 11 were condemned to death (including Hermann Goering, who escaped hanging by suicide). The pursuit and punishment of the many lesser Nazis involved in the 'final solution' continues to this day.

Behind the wire, men and women were segregated, families divided. Prisoners wore coloured patches to denote their 'crimes'.

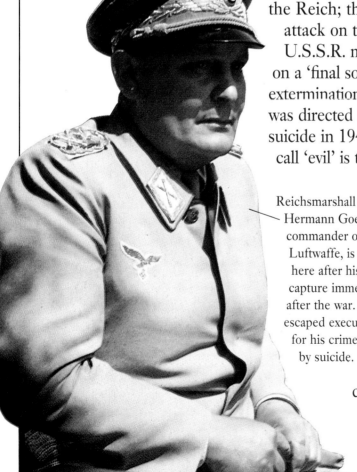

Reichsmarshall Hermann Goering, commander of the Luftwaffe, is seen here after his capture immediately after the war. He escaped execution for his crimes by suicide.

A survivor of Buchenwald. This concentration camp in central Germany was infamous for vile 'medical experiments' carried out on its inmates.

This heap of emaciated bodies represents just a few of an estimated 60,000 who died in Buchenwald – and a tiny fraction of the millions murdered in other camps.

Nazi leaders accused of war crimes face the judgment of an international military tribunal at Nuremberg in November 1945.

Hess   Ribbentrop   Keitel

Dönitz   Raeder   Schirach   Sauckel

Rosenberg

Goering

FACT FILE

❑ Mass murder of Jews began before the official adoption of the 'final solution', at the Wannsee Conference, Berlin, January 1942. In Poland and the U.S.S.R., S.S. *Einsatzgruppen* ('Action Squads') forced Jews into vehicles whose exhaust pipes had been ducted into airtight interiors, where they died by slow suffocation.

❑ In 1940, c.450,000 Jews were penned in the Warsaw Ghetto (below), from which they were taken for extermination. On April 19, 1943, the survivors (c.60,000, but only c.1,500 armed) rose under the 'Star of David' flag. For 28 days they held off S.S. troops under General Jürgen Stroop: c.14,000 Jews died fighting, but the Ghetto was razed and its last inhabitants sent to death camps. Postwar, Stroop was condemned to death by a U.S. court, for atrocities in Greece, and by a Polish court for his crimes in Warsaw – where he was hanged in 1951.

Leyte Gulf: the greatest sea battle

These 406mm (16in) guns fired for the last time at Leyte Gulf, in history's last clash between battleships.

On October 20, 1944, Admiral Kinkaid's U.S. 7th Fleet landed General Krueger's 6th Army on the east coast of Leyte, Philippines. Two days later, making good his promise of 1942, General MacArthur waded ashore there. The I.J.N. committed all its remaining strength to the destruction of the invasion fleet. On October 23-26, 65 Japanese and 166 Allied (two Australian) warships fought the largest naval engagement in history: four battles together known as Leyte Gulf. U.S. planes sank the super-battleship *Musashi* in the Sibuyan Sea, but then Admiral Halsey's heavy carriers went in pursuit of Admiral Ozawa's carrier fleet – a decoy force almost bare of aircraft. Ozawa's carriers were sunk off Cape Engano, but in Halsey's absence Admiral Kurita's battleships and cruisers were able to strike at the invasion fleet off Samar. U.S. destroyers gallantly opposed his advance, and fearing that Halsey would trap him, Kurita fled. Admiral Nishimura's Southern Force was destroyed by Kinkaid in Surigao Strait – history's last battleship-versus-battleship action. The I.J.N. lost 4 carriers, 3 battleships, 10 cruisers and 11 destroyers; the U.S.N., 3 carriers (one to *kamikaze* air attack) and 3 destroyers. Reconquest of the Philippines was assured – but it took hard fighting ashore. Leyte was secured in December, at a cost of c.16,000 U.S. casualties. On January 9 1945, U.S. 6th Army landed on Luzon, defended by c.260,000 Japanese under General Yamashita, who hoped by prolonged resistance to delay the invasion of Japan. He did not surrender until August 1945: U.S. losses on Luzon were c.8,000 dead and 33,000 wounded; Japanese dead exceeded 190,000.

'I shall return!' MacArthur keeps the promise made in 1942 as he wades ashore on Leyte Island in October 1944.

The Japanese would fight savagely for Leyte. Some 60,000 died there; only 400 became prisoners.

Scarred by bomb damage, the Japanese battleship *Nagato* is seen at anchor at the war's end.

A U.S.N. transport is dwarfed by the 39,000 tonne bulk of the surrendered battleship.

❑ Admiral William ('Bull') Halsey (above) (1882-1959) was given to such signals as: 'Kill more Japs!'; 'Keep the bastards dying!' His aggression did much for victory in the Pacific – but his recklessness almost led to disaster at Leyte Gulf. On the day of Japan's surrender, suspecting a final *kamikaze* effort, he ordered that 'snooping' planes should be shot out of the sky 'in a friendly sort of way'.

❑ General Yamashita, in command on Luzon, ordered that Manila, capital of the Philippines, should not be defended. He hoped to spare its population – but he was disobeyed by Admiral Iwabuchi, whose 19,000 troops waged a savage house-to-house battle, laying the city in ruins and killing c.100,000 civilians. Iwabuchi was killed in action; Yamashita's execution for 'war crimes' (notably Manila) in 1946 has been denounced by Western historians as a gross injustice.

Spotless 'whites' distinguish MacArthur and his staff, as the Supreme Allied Commander, Southwest Pacific, inspects the Leyte beachhead.

Landing craft carry men of General Krueger's U.S. 6th Army from the invasion armada to the first foothold in the reconquest of the Philippines.

Kamikaze: the divine wind

'Duty is heavier than a mountain; death lighter than a feather,' declared Emperor Mutsuhito in 1882. His words guided Japan's suicide forces – the *kamikaze* ('divine wind': from a typhoon that destroyed a Mongol invasion fleet in the 13th century). Many Japanese fought suicidally throughout the war, but 'official' *kamikaze* units were not formed until October 1944. Then, because of a lack of planes and veteran flyers in the Philippines, pilots volunteered to crash-dive bomb-laden planes on to Allied warships. On October 25, at Leyte Gulf, the first *kamikaze* attacks sank the escort carrier USS *St Lo* and badly damaged other ships. At Okinawa, March-August 1945, *kamikaze* planes sank 20 Allied ships and damaged 217: non-suicidal air attacks sank only 6 and damaged 45. According to Japanese figures, 2,409 I.J.N. and 2,206 I.J.A. pilots died as *kamikaze*. Another suicidal air weapon was the *ohka* ('cherry blossom'), a piloted, rocket powered bomb launched from a 'mother' plane. Its undersea equivalent was the *kaiten* ('turn to heaven'), a manned version of the 'Long Lance' torpedo. Some 150 *kaiten* were launched from submarines and surface ships, sinking two U.S. warships and damaging five. Explosive motorboats (*shinyo*, 'ocean shakers') made many suicidal ramming attacks on Allied invasion forces, sinking some 10 landing ships. On land, soldiers facing certain defeat made '*banzai* charges' – suicidal attacks to ensure 'honourable' death in action. In August 1945, more than 5,300 *kamikaze* planes, 4,000 *shinyo*, 500 *kaiten* and midget submarines, and many *ohka*, were deployed in Japan against the expected Allied invasion fleet.

A pillar of fire and smoke marks the steep, final attacking dive of a hard hit Japanese *kamikaze* aircraft.

Aircraft carriers were the prime targets for *kamikaze* attack. Unlike British carriers, U.S.N. carriers did not have armoured flight decks.

Lone suicide planes could seldom penetrate air cover and A.A.A. Mass attacks were more successful.

A *shinyo* explosive motor boat captured at Okinawa. These frail, wooden, one-man craft, powered by automobile engines, were used for suicidal ramming attacks.

A *shinyo's* 'sting' lay beneath this forward hatch. Its bow was packed with up to 300kg (660lb) of explosive, fused to explode on impact. The boats usually attacked in large groups.

More than 4,000 Japanese aircraft were expended as *kamikaze* – and some 5,000 more were ready in Japan to meet an Allied invasion that never came. Most ended in 'graveyards' like this one.

The Mitsubishi A6M 'Zero,' one of the war's finest fighters, was adapted to carry a 250kg (500lb) or 500kg (1,100lb) bomb in *kamikaze* attacks.

❏ Japan built several extra large (*STo* class) submarines equipped with aircraft hangars (above). They hoped to launch Aichi M6A1 *Seiran* seaplane-bombers to make *kamikaze* attacks on targets within the U.S.A., or, as planned in May 1945, on the Panama Canal.

❏ The first *kamikaze* air units were formed by Admiral Takijiro Onishi, who had been one of the major planners of the Pearl Harbor attack. On Japan's surrender, he committed *seppuku* (ritual suicide) in accordance with the *samurai* tradition.

❏ The *ohka* piloted bomb was called the *baka* ('idiot') by the Allies. Its 'mother' plane, the Mitsubishi G4M 'Betty' bomber, was so unwieldy when carrying it that most were shot down by Allied fighters before they could launch their missiles.

❏ The first line in the suicidal defense of Japan itself was held by *fukuryu* ('crouching dragon') frogmen. They were to march along the sea bed to destroy landing craft with pole-mounted explosives.

Stepping stones to Tokyo

The Chance Vought F4U Corsair single seat fighter was used by the Allies for both carrier and land based operations.

Final 'stepping stones' in the Allied advance on Japan were the islands of Iwo Jima, needed as a base for U.S. fighters to escort B-29s raiding Japan, and Okinawa, only c.650km (400mi) south of Tokyo. U.S. Marines landed on Iwo Jima on February 19, 1945. The beaches were lightly defended – but inland General Kuribayashi's 23,000 strong garrison had made the tiny (21sq km/8sq mi) island a maze of blockhouses, tunnels and caverns, centring on Mount Suribachi. Kuribayashi ordered: 'Regard your position as your grave . . . No man must die until he has killed 10 enemies.' It took c.85,000 Marines (who suffered c.7,000 killed and 17,000 wounded) to prize out the defenders with explosives, flamethrowers and cold steel. Only 1,080 Japanese survived on March 27, when resistance ended with Kuribayashi's suicide. On April 1, General Buckner's U.S. 10th Army landed in southwest Okinawa. General Ushijima had concentrated most of his 120,000 men in a triple ring of 'Shuri Line' fortifications around his HQ at Shuri Castle. U.S. Marines had cleared northern Okinawa by April 20, but to the south the Japanese held out in the Shuri Line's caves and tunnels. Shuri Castle fell on May 29 and Ushijima, after a last stand in the south, committed suicide on June 20. More than 100,000 Japanese died on Okinawa; only c.8,000 surrendered. U.S. Army and Marine losses were c.7,600 dead and 32,000 wounded. The U.S.N. also lost heavily: 26 warships were sunk and 262 damaged (c.4,900 killed; 4,800 wounded), most by *kamikaze* attack, and c.780 aircraft lost.

A Japanese soldier holds aloft the white flag of surrender. This was a sight rarely seen in the Pacific. True to the ancient *bushido* code, most Japanese fought to the death.

Only towards the war's end did unwounded Japanese surrender in large groups: as seen here on Okinawa in June 1945. Even so, only c.8,000 Japanese surrendered on Okinawa; more than 100,000 died fighting or suicided.

A salvo of 127mm (5in) rockets streaks from a U.S. Marine Corps' F4U Corsair towards a target on Okinawa.

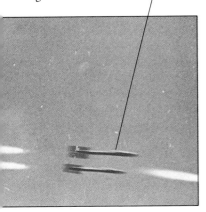

U.S. Marines use flamethrowers against Japanese bunkers at Mount Suribachi, Iwo Jima. The M1/M2 Flamethrower, weighing c.32kg (70lb) with a 15l (3.3gal) backpack of fuel, shot a jet of fire to c.9-14m (30-45yd) for some 10 seconds. Then bulldozers moved in to entomb Japanese who had survived cremation or suffocation.

The map is a locator for events described on *pages 90-99.* U.S. forces landed in the Philippines; then took Iwo Jima and Okinawa. Bombers from the Marianas blasted Japanese cities. In August 1945, the Soviets invaded Manchuria.

Map labels: U.S.S.R., MANCHURIA, KOREA, JAPAN, Tokyo, Hiroshima, Nagasaki, CHINA, PACIFIC OCEAN, Okinawa, Iwo Jima, PHILIPPINE ISLANDS, Manila, Mariana Islands, Leyte Gulf

FACT FILE

❏ Japan lost more than 7,000 planes at Okinawa: c.2,000 of them as *kamikaze* in 10 mass attacks, causing devastation like that aboard USS *Bunker Hill* (below). The super-battleship *Yamato*, on a one-way mission to run aground on Okinawa and become a 'land fortress', was sunk by U.S. planes en route. More effective were anti-tank suicide squads: on the Shuri Line, April 19, U.S. 193rd Tank Battalion lost six M4 Shermans to soldiers with 10kg (22lb) explosive charges strapped to their bodies, who flung themselves beneath the American tanks.

❏ The photograph, 'Raising Old Glory on Iwo Jima', taken by Joseph Rosenthal, inspired the U.S.M.C.'s War Memorial at Arlington, Va. But it does not show the original incident. The first flag hoisted by the Marines was too small to be seen from the beaches. The U.S.N. provided a larger one, which for Rosenthal's famous picture was raised by five Marines and a sailor.

'Back to the Stone Age'

U.S. bombs first fell on Japan on April 18, 1942, when 16 B-25 Mitchell bombers took off from the carrier USS *Hornet* to attack Tokyo and nearby military targets. Attempting afterwards to reach bases in China, 15 planes were lost (three flyers were executed by the Japanese), but the heroic mission, commanded by Lieutenant Colonel James H. Doolittle, was a great morale booster. Strategic bombing began from bases in China in June 1944; then conquest of the Marianas provided bases that put all Japan within range of B-29 Superfortresses. In November 1944, B-29s began 'precision' attacks against Japanese factories. General Curtis LeMay, head of XXI Bomber Command from January 1945, believed 'area bombing' of industrial cities was more effective. Stripping his B-29s of guns (for extra speed) and loading them with incendiaries, he launched low-level night attacks by huge formations that overwhelmed Japan's A.A.A. and fighter defences. On March 9-10, 1945, in the war's most destructive air raid, 325 B-29s hit Tokyo: a fire storm burned out 41sq km (15.8sq mi) of the city and killed or injured c.183,000 people. In the next fortnight, 'fire raids' destroyed the industrial centres of Nagoya, Osaka and Kobe. LeMay promised to 'bomb Japan back into the Stone Age'. By August 1945, U.S. 20th Air Force had dropped c.104,000 tonnes of bombs in some 15,000 sorties, losing c.400 B-29s in combat. About 330,000 Japanese were killed and 500,000 injured; 42 per cent of the total area of 66 Japanese cities was devastated. Strategic bombing was a final blow to a war economy already crippled by the U.S. submarine and aerial minelaying campaigns against merchant shipping.

'Jimmy' Doolittle led the first bombing raid on Tokyo, launched from a U.S. Navy carrier, in April 1942.

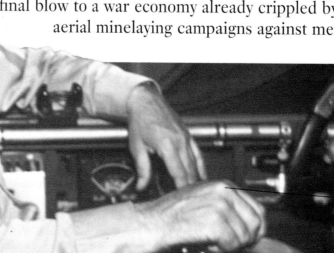

Clusters of incendiaries tumble from U.S. bombers over Japan, where 'fire raids' proved more damaging than high explosive bombing.

Later in the war, Doolittle was promoted to Lieutenant General and commanded U.S. 8th Air Force in Europe.

The mighty Boeing B-29 Superfortress came late to the war, flying its first combat mission in June 1944. By 1945, formations of up to 500 Superfortresses were reducing Japan to ashes.

Stripped of defensive armament, B-29s flew fast and fairly low to drop their deadly bomb loads.

This was Tokyo in mid-1945, when U.S. bombers had completely destroyed about one-half of all the Japanese capital's buildings.

Fire has obliterated all traditional wood-built structures – and of modern, steel-framed buildings, only the burned out shells still stand.

❏ Maintaining wartime secrecy, President Roosevelt told press men that the 'Doolittle Raid' bombers flew from 'Shangri-La' (a Tibetan utopia in the best-selling novel *Lost Horizon*). In tribute to Doolittle and his men, an aircraft carrier launched in February 1944 was named USS *Shangri-La*.

❏ In late 1944 Japan launched its '*Fu-Go*' bombing offensive at the U.S.A. About 9,300 layered paper hydrogen balloons of 10.6m (35ft) diameter were launched in Honshu to drift c.9,700km (6,000mi) to the U.S. mainland. Each carried three small bombs. The only victims were a woman and five children at Lakeview, Oregon, May 5, 1945.

❏ Only one Japanese aircraft bombed the U.S. mainland. In August-September 1942 a small Yokosuka 'Glen' seaplane launched from the submarine *I-25* twice dropped incendiary bombs in Oregon, hoping to start forest fires.

❏ The Boeing B-29 Superfortress was the heaviest combat aircraft of the war, weighing more than 45 tonnes fully loaded and with a wingspan of 43m (141ft). It could carry up to 8,712 kg (20,000lb) of bombs over a combat range of more than 6,440km (4,000mi). Some 400 B-29s were lost during the bombing offensive against Japan in 1944-1945.

'Little Boy' and 'Fat Man'

From early 1945 Allied commanders planned 'Operation Downfall', the invasion of Japan. Two assaults were scheduled: 'Olympic' in November 1945; 'Coronet' in March 1946. Japan's home defence slogan was 'One hundred million will die for Emperor and Nation!', and U.S. commanders believed Allied casualties might exceed 250,000. This was a major reason for President Truman's decision to use a new and terrible weapon, the nuclear ('atomic') bomb. Scientists who had fled Hitler's tyranny played a large part in the Allied atomic programme, while Germany's atomic research centres were destroyed by commando raids and precision bombing. A nuclear weapon was developed by the U.S. Army's 'Manhattan Project', with Dr. Robert Oppenheimer as scientific director, from September 1942. On July 16, 1945, the 'nuclear age' began with a test explosion at Alamogordo, N. Mex. Early on August 6, 1945, a B-29 from Tinian, Marianas, dropped the first atomic (uranium) bomb on Hiroshima.

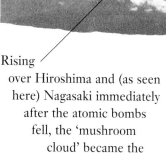

Rising over Hiroshima and (as seen here) Nagasaki immediately after the atomic bombs fell, the 'mushroom cloud' became the sinister symbol of the nuclear age.

The 3m (10ft) long, 4,080kg (9,000lb) 'Little Boy' detonated above the city centre: c.78,000 people died instantly; about the same number suffered horrific burns or absorbed 'radiation' that would later kill or cripple them. On August 9, a second (plutonium) bomb, 'Fat Man', killed c.40,000 at Nagasaki – while the U.S.S.R., having declared war on Japan on August 8, poured c.1,200,000 troops into Manchukuo. Emperor Hirohito, announcing Japan's surrender to his people on August 15, spoke of 'new and most cruel' weapons, but the atomic bombs, by allowing Japan to surrender with some semblance of 'honour', saved tens of thousands of Japanese, as well as Allied, lives.

A 'Little Boy' atomic bomb: the nuclear device used at Hiroshima on August 6, 1945. Within the bomb, conventional explosive blasted together two pieces of Uranium 235, producing a chain reaction that caused an explosion equivalent to 20,000 tons of T.N.T.

'Fat Man', used at Nagasaki, had about the same power as 'Little Boy', but used plutonium, set off by an 'implosion' of conventional explosive (T.N.T.), rather than uranium. Slightly longer (3.2m/10.7ft) but much fatter (1.5m/5ft, against 0.7m/2.3ft) than 'Little Boy', it weighed c.4,536kg (10,000lb).

The great 'fire storm' generated at ground level by the bomb's explosion sucks in air which is thrust aloft in a column of smoke and ashes.

Civilians walk among the ruins of Hiroshima. Death caused by the atomic bomb did not end when the fires burned out: in years to come, thousands more would die from the effects of radiation.

❑ Many scientists, including Oppenheimer (who in the 1950s would be persecuted for his 'leftist' views), opposed the use of the atomic bomb on a 'live' target. The great Albert Einstein (1879-1955) said: 'If I had known [that my work would contribute to the bomb's development] I would rather have been a simple locksmith.'

❑ 'Enola Gay' (below), the B-29 from which the bomb was dropped on Hiroshima, was named by its pilot (centre), Colonel Paul W. Tibbets, Jr. (b.1915), after his mother.

❑ The Hiroshima bomb is estimated to have had an explosive power equal to that of 10,000 four-engined bombers of the time all dropping their conventional bomb loads on the same spot at the same moment.

❑ On August 22, Japan's Kwantung Army in Manchukuo surrendered to the Soviets and Chinese. Soviet forces suffered c.31,000 casualties, and took some 600,000 Japanese prisoners, many of whom died in labour camps.

SUPERFACTS

Worst war loss ▼
Proportionately, Poland suffered the worst loss of any country in World War II: 6,000,000 dead, or about 18 per cent of her 1939 population (below). Some 50 per cent of the Polish dead were Jews.

Reichstag fire
Anti-Communist hysteria in Germany in 1933-34 helped make Hitler dictator. It was fuelled by the 'Reichstag Fire' of February 27, 1933. Marianus van der Lubbe, tried and executed for setting the torch to the German parliament building, implicated a number of German Communists in the act, but many historians believe that the mentally-ill Dutchman was a Nazi tool.

The first 'blitzkrieg'
In May-August 1939 Japan's Kwantung Army, seeking to expand its Chinese puppet-state of Manchukuo, clashed with Soviet forces at Nomonhan on the Outer Mongolian border. In a 10-day action, Red Army General Zhukov used bombers as 'flying artillery', flame-throwing tanks (and Mongolian horsed cavalry) to inflict some 20,000 casualties on the Japanese and drive them back into Manchuria. Zhukov's early use of *blitzkrieg* tactics was ignored in the West.

First air raid warning ▼
Wailing sirens delivered Britain's first air raid warning only 15 minutes after her declaration of war on September 3, 1939 (below). It was a false alarm. Soon, total 'black out', with all lights at night forbidden, led to many highway accidents. The wild ponies of the New Forest in southern England were involved in

so many collisions that an attempt was made to paint them with zebra stripes.

Longest serving military arm
The U.S. Colt .45 Model 1911 automatic pistol was the standard sidearm of U.S. services through World Wars I and II and until the late 1980s, when it was replaced by the 9mm Beretta Model 92F pistol. Colt produced more than 3,000,000; other manufacturers, many more.

First shots of World War II
They were fired at 0440 hours on September 1, 1939, when the old (1906) German battleship *Schleswig-Holstein* bombarded a Polish fort in Danzig harbour.

Naked warriors
Witches and warlocks claimed credit for stopping Germany's invasion of Britain! On August 1, 1940, male and female occultists gathered in southern England to create a 'cone of power'. In a 'skyclad' (naked) ritual, they 'beamed' messages to Hitler: 'You cannot cross the sea'; 'You cannot succeed.'

Youngest general
German fighter pilot Adolf Galland (b.1912) downed 103 enemy

planes during World War II, some 50 of them during the 'Battle of Britain'. In 1941 he became Germany's youngest (29) general. But when Goering asked what his pilots most needed for victory, Galland is said to have replied: 'A few squadrons of Spitfires!'

Japanese-Americans at home
Soon after the Pearl Harbor attack, 'invasion fever' on the U.S. west coast caused the evacuation of c.115,000 Americans of Japanese descent to War Relocation Authority internment camps well inland. Many lost all their possessions; a few were lynched. But most were loyal to the U.S.A., and early in 1943 U.S. Army Chief of Staff General Marshall headed moves to restore their constitutional rights.

. . . and at war
One of the hardest-fighting U.S. units in European operations was the 442nd Regimental Combat Team, which won four Distinguished Unit Citations, more than 18,000 individual medals, and incurred some 9, 500 casualties (or three times its strength 'on paper'). Except for its most senior officers, the 442nd R.C.T. was composed entirely of Japanese-Americans (*Nisei*).

Unhappy ending
The cruiser USS *Phoenix* survived the attack on Pearl Harbor and later weathered the great battle of Leyte Gulf and *kamikaze* attacks with only minor damage. In 1951 she was sold to Argentina, and later renamed *General Belgrano*. On May 2, 1982, during the Falklands War caused by Argentina's attempt to take the islands, she was torpedoed and sunk (368 dead) by the British submarine HMS *Conqueror*.

Americans against war
Until Pearl Harbor, most Americans (so polls showed) opposed the U.S.A.'s involvement in a European war. The slogan 'OHIO' was used by protestors of the Selective Service Act, requiring draftees to report for service in October 1941. Chalked on walls nationwide, it meant 'Over the Hill [i.e., 'make yourself scarce'] In October'.

Most bloody battle
German and Soviet military and civilian deaths at Stalingrad may have exceeded 2,000,000. The city's pre-war population of c.520,000 had fallen to fewer than 2,000 by January 1943.

'Gangster gun' ▷
The U.S. Army took into service the famous Thompson sub-machine gun (right) in 1938 – but when it was offered to the British Army, traditionally minded officers objected to equipping their men with 'gangster weapons'. After 1939, Britain bought as many 'tommy guns' as she could get. In all, about 1,400,000 Thompsons were produced.

Fastest aircraft ▽
The fastest aircraft to enter combat in World War II was Germany's Messerschmitt Me 163 *Komet* ('Comet') rocket fighter (below), with a top speed of

c.960kmh (596mph) – but with fuel endurance of only 90 seconds and a range of only c.96km (60mi).

Disabled 'aces'
Group Captain Douglas Bader (1910-82), distinguished British fighter commander in the 'Battle of Britain', conquered the loss of both legs in 1931 to become a fine combat pilot. One of Japan's greatest 'aces', Lieutenant Saburo Sakai (b.1916), scored many of his 64 'kills' after losing an eye in combat over Guadalcanal in 1942.

SUPERFACTS

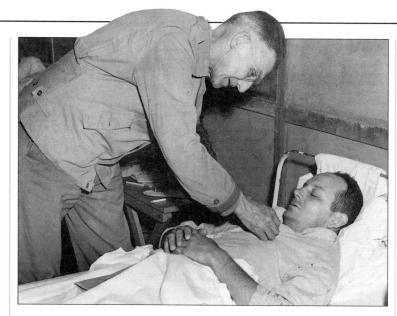

Heaviest tank
The heaviest tank ever was the German *Maus* ('Mouse'), first tested in late 1943. Massively armoured, it weighed 188 tonnes, mounted one 127mm (5in) and one 76mm (3in) gun, and had a top speed of 20kmh (12.5mph). Only a few were made; they saw no combat. Nor did the heaviest U.S. armoured vehicle, the 90 tonne T28, mounting a 105mm (4.1in) gun and with armour up to 305mm (12in) thick.

Heaviest combat tank
In World War II this was the German PzKw.VI Tiger II (*Königstiger*; 'King Tiger'). Weighing 68 tonnes, with armour up to 185mm (7.3in) thick, it mounted an 88mm (3.5in) gun and had a road speed of 39kmh (24mph). Some 480 entered service in 1944-45.

Women in combat
More than 1,000 women served as combat aircrew with the Red Air Force. Soviet sources credit women fighter pilots with 125 air combats and 38 'kills'. Leading female 'ace', with 12 victories, was Lieutenant Lily Litvak (right), the 'Rose of Stalingrad', killed in action in 1943.

Sharp-tongued general
Plain-speaking U.S. General Stilwell (above left) was nicknamed 'Vinegar Joe'. Hailed for inspiring leadership after saving his Chinese troops from destruction in Burma in 1942, he said only 'I claim we took a hell of a beating.' He detested Chinese Nationalist leader Chiang Kai-shek, whom he called 'The Peanut', and suggested that for military purposes the U.S.A. should support the Chinese Communists led by Chu Teh and Mao Tse-tung.

Heaviest gun
'Gustav', Germany's 80cm (31.5in) K(E) railway gun, was the heaviest artillery piece of all time. It had a 30m (95ft) barrel, weighed 1, 350 tonnes, and fired a 4.7 tonne shell to a range of 47km (29mi). Special trains transported the dismantled gun and the 1, 420 men needed to assemble, operate and guard it. It fired only a few times, at the siege of Sevastopol, Crimea, in 1941.

British fascist
One of Mussolini's greatest admirers was British politician Sir Oswald Mosley (1896-1980). A former socialist cabinet minister, he returned from a visit to Italy in 1932 to found his own 'Blackshirts', the British Union of Fascists. Mosley and some of his followers were imprisoned in Britain during World War II.

Biggest war memorial
The Soviet victory at Stalingrad (now Volgograd) in 1942-43 is commemorated by what is said to be the world's tallest statue. The 'Motherland' figure erected in the 1960s measures 82m (270ft) from its base to the tip of its uplifted sword.

Most perilous sea route
The 'Murmansk Run', the Arctic convoy route from Britain to the Soviet Union, was perhaps the most dangerous sea lane of World War II. In July 1942, Convoy PQ-17 lost 24 of its 35 ships to U-boats and bombers. Allied materiel delivered to Russia in 1942-45 included some 13,000 tanks, 22,000 planes and 376,000 trucks.

Death penalty
On January 31, 1945, Private Eddie Slovik was the only U.S. soldier of World War II (and the first since the Civil War) to be executed for desertion in the face of the enemy. Poor Slovik, a near illiterate loner, appears to have been chosen as an 'example' by officers worried at an increasing desertion rate.

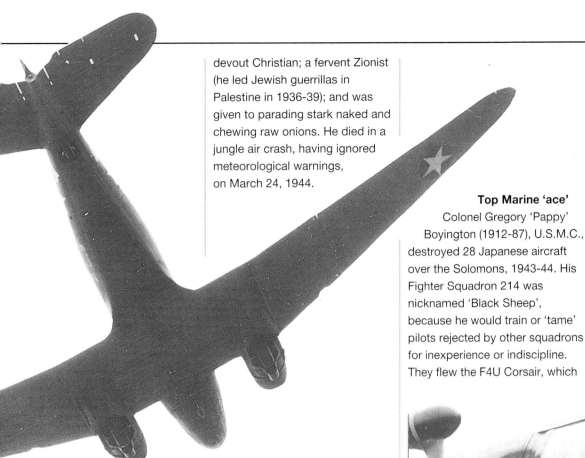

devout Christian; a fervent Zionist (he led Jewish guerrillas in Palestine in 1936-39); and was given to parading stark naked and chewing raw onions. He died in a jungle air crash, having ignored meteorological warnings, on March 24, 1944.

Top Marine 'ace'
Colonel Gregory 'Pappy' Boyington (1912-87), U.S.M.C., destroyed 28 Japanese aircraft over the Solomons, 1943-44. His Fighter Squadron 214 was nicknamed 'Black Sheep', because he would train or 'tame' pilots rejected by other squadrons for inexperience or indiscipline. They flew the F4U Corsair, which the Japanese nicknamed the 'Whistling Death'.

'V' for victory
Simple but effective, the 'V for Victory' campaign expressed western Europe's opposition to Nazi occupation forces. The 'V' sign (below) was chalked on walls and tapped out or whistled in Morse code. The Morse 'V' (dot-dot-dot-dash) echoed the opening bars of Beethoven's 5th Symphony, used as a call sign by the British Broadcasting Corporation's European Service, which transmitted anti-Nazi propaganda to the continent.

Black pilots
In 1941-45, many black U.S.A.A.F. pilots trained at Tuskegee, Ala., where, because of segregation, they were nicknamed 'Lonely Eagles'. First commander of an all-black air combat unit was Lieutenant Colonel Benjamin O. Davis, Jr. (b.1912; in 1954 he became the U.S.A.F.'s first black three-star general). His father, Brigadier General Benjamin O. Davis, Sr. (1877-1970), had become the U.S. Army's first black general in 1940.

'Chindit' leader
Eccentric British Major General Orde Wingate (1903-44) organized the 'Chindits' (named for the *chinthe*, a lion-like figure that guards Burmese temples) for commando raids behind Japanese lines in Burma. A manic-depressive who twice attempted suicide, he was a

Most useful aircraft
General Eisenhower called the Douglas C-47 Skytrain (Dakota) all-purpose transport aircraft (above), 'one of the most significant weapons of World War II.' The prototype of this long-lived workhorse flew in 1935; some 10,000 had been built by 1945; they saw service as gun-ships ('Puff the Magic Dragon') in Vietnam in the 1960s; and many hundreds are still flying.

Heaviest mortars
The heaviest mortars (short barrelled guns, for high angle fire) ever fired in combat were German '*Karl*' howitzers used in the sieges of Soviet cities. Able to move for short distances on caterpillar tracks, the 124 tonne, 600mm (23.6in) calibre '*Karl*' hurled a 2.2 tonne concrete piercing shell to a range of 4.5km (2.8mi). The U.S. Army developed a 915mm (36in) mortar, 'Little David', intended for use against fortifications in Japan.

SUPERFACTS

Iceberg airstrips

'Habbakuk', a plan to provide air cover for convoys, received considerable British attention from 1942. It called for the construction of huge artificial 'icebergs' – ice bonded with wood fibre – as self-propelled landing strips in the North Atlantic.

Dickensian nickname

Scientists are still sometimes called 'Boffins'. The name is said to have originated in World War II, when scientists at an R.A.F. research establishment were given nicknames from the novels of Charles Dickens. 'Mr Boffin' is a character in the novel *Our Mutual Friend*.

Allied insults ▼

The high pay, smart uniforms and generous rations of U.S. servicemen stationed in Britain (below) aroused the envy of

British troops, who complained the 'Yanks' were 'Overpaid, oversexed, overfed – and over here.' The G.I.s countered that the 'Limeys' were 'Underpaid, underfed, undersexed – and under Eisenhower' (Allied supremo in Europe after 1942).

The durable 'Jeep' ▲

A famous wartime vehicle was the quarter-ton, four-wheel-drive, command and reconnaissance car – the 'Jeep' (above) – developed by Willys for U.S. forces. Its name came from its 'General Purpose' designation, and from 'Eugene the Jeep', a versatile character in the 'Popeye' comic. Some 640,000 Jeeps were built in 1941-45 and many more later, into the 1990s.

Radio traitors

'Tokyo Rose' was the name given by G.I.s to various Japanese-American girls who made propaganda broadcasts from Tokyo. Best known was Iva Ikuko Toguri d'Aquino (b.1916), who served six years' imprisonment after the war.

Rest and recreation

In 1939 the Entertainments National Service Association (E.N.S.A.; nicknamed 'Every Night Something Awful') was set up to provide entertainment for British

servicemen. It put on 1,016,214 performances during World War II. Its U.S. equivalent, the United Service Organizations (U.S.O.), is estimated to have had more than 1 billion customers in 1941-45.

Highest ranking officer killed

In World War II the highest ranking U.S. officer to die in action was Lieutenant General Simon Bolivar Buckner (1886-1945), commanding 10th Army in the invasion of Okinawa. The son of a Confederate States Army general, he led from the front, and on June 18, 1945, at a forward observation post, was struck in the heart by a shell splinter.

Youngest killed: oldest soldier

The youngest British combatant killed in action in World War II is believed to be Galley Boy (Merchant Navy) R.V. Steed, aged 14 on April 26, 1943, when his ship struck a mine. He is buried in a military cemetery in Casablanca. Next to him lies Field Marshal Sir Claude Auchinleck (1884-1981), who died at the age of 96 as Britain's oldest serving soldier (British Field Marshals never 'officially' retire).

Two tricksters

In 1942 the Dutch artist Hans van Meegeren acted as agent in the sale of a great art treasure, Vermeer's painting '*Woman Taken in Adultery*', to Hermann Goering. Post-war, when van Meegeren was accused of collaboration with the Nazis, it emerged, first, that he was an expert forger who had painted the 'masterpiece' himself; second, that Goering had paid for it with forged currency.

Leading 'pin up girl'

The war's top 'pin up' was movie actress Betty Grable (1916-73). In 1943-45, G.I.s requested a photograph showing her in a swimsuit, with her 'Million Dollar Legs' clad in fishnet tights, at a rate of more than 20,000 copies per week.

History's biggest air force

By mid-1944 the U.S.A.A.F. was the biggest air arm the world has ever seen, with c.79, 910 planes and 2, 411,000 personnel.

Most decorated U.S. soldier

This is said to have been U.S. Army Lieutenant Audie Murphy (1924-71), awarded the Medal of Honor and 27 other decorations. Post-war, Murphy starred in some 40 movies, including the story of his own war experiences, *To Hell and Back* (1955).

Longest surviving Nazi leader

This was Rudolf Hess (1894-1987), Hitler's one-time deputy, who in 1941 fled to England (perhaps hoping to negotiate peace). Sentenced at Nuremberg

to life imprisonment, Hess was held at Spandau prison, Berlin, where he committed suicide at the age of 92. Some say he was 'helped' to die by his gaolers, to whom he had become an 'embarrassment'.

Only helicopter in action

Although both Allies and Axis possessed rotor aircraft, only one true helicopter saw combat service in World War II. In March 1944, Lieutenant Carter Harman, U.S.A.A.F., in a Sikorsky R-4B helicopter, made four flights from an Allied base in Burma to pick up wounded commandos from a paddy field.

'Mae West' and 'Bazooka' ▼

Two World War II inventions named for popular entertainers were the R.A.F.'s inflatable lifejacket (below), worn around the chest, which took its name from the big-bosomed movie actress Mae West; and the U.S. Army's 60mm (2.36in) anti-tank rocket launcher, the 'bazooka', (below right) after a weird musical instrument played by comedian Bob Burns. The Red Army's *Katyusha* rocket mortar, usually used in multiple assemblies, was called by the Germans 'Stalin's Organ'.

Funny money

In 'Operation *Bernhard*', planned by Himmler, engravers and printers held in concentration camps were 'persuaded' to forge British bank notes to the value of about £140 million (then $600 million). The plan to damage Britain's economy by putting them into circulation was abandoned in 1944.

Greatest understatement

Emperor Hirohito's surrender broadcast of August 15, 1945, contained one of history's greatest understatements. The phrase, said to have been suggested by Minister of War Korechika Anami (who committed suicide just before the broadcast) was 'the war has developed not necessarily to Japan's advantage'.

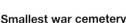

Smallest war cemetery

The smallest cemetery maintained by the British Commonwealth War Graves Commission lies on Ocracoke Island, North Carolina. It is the resting place of four British sailors from the armed trawler HMS *Bedfordshire*, torpedoed off the Outer Banks by a U-boat on May 11, 1942.

Page numbers in **bold** indicate major references including accompanying photographs. Page numbers in *italics* indicate captions to illustrations. Other entries are in normal type.

U.S. forces prepare for the liberation of Europe, Spring 1944. During rehearsals for the Normandy invasion, an Army truck is loaded aboard a U.S. Navy Tank Landing Ship (LST).